PAULL: An illustrated history

David Alexander Smith

ISBN 9781840335361

**The publishers regret that they cannot supply
copies of any pictures featured in this book.**

Contents

Chapter 1: In The Beginning   3

Chapter 2: Houses of Significance   6

Chapter 3: In Defence of the Realm   20

Chapter 4: Lighthouses   36

Chapter 5: Religion   41

Chapter 6: Public Houses   57

Chapter 7: Cork Models and Skeletons: Battersby's museum at Paull   60

Chapter 8: Trades and Occupations   63

Chapter 9: Paull Workhouse   65

Chapter 10: Paull Airfield   67

Chapter 11: Paull at the Start of the 21st Century   70

Bibliography   75

Index   77

Acknowledgements

This book could not have been written without the help of the Hull Local Studies Library (now at the Hull History Centre) where much of the information has been found. I would also like to thank the following organisations for their help in finding information: Hull City Archives; the Beverley Local Studies Library; Sarah Acton and the Staff of East Riding of Yorkshire Archives; the Borthwick Institute of Historical Research, University of York; and the East Yorkshire Family History Society for the information on monumental inscriptions and parish registers.

Thanks are also due to the following people who have helped with information on the history of Paull: Margaret Oliver for the information on Paull workhouse; the ladies who look after the church on its open days for their information; Helen Godwin; Arthur and Mary Credland; Martin Craven; Philip Hampel; Alan Brigham; Bryan Elletson.

CHAPTER 1: IN THE BEGINNING
Origins

This plan showing the River Humber from Hull to just beyond Paull around 1580 is probably the earliest view of Paull in existence and labels Paull Holme showing the house there with two towers. In 1887 the Hull publisher M.C. Peck & Son sold copies of this map adapted from the original in the British Museum. Peck described it as a "quaint" and "curious" map of Holderness that "…was doubtless prepared in anticipation of the threatened attack by the Spanish Armada." The map (it may be more accurate to call it a chart) was in fact commissioned by Lord Burghley, the Secretary of State for Elizabeth I and it was created to help repel an invading force. Burghley's chart shows Paull located just four and a half miles east of Hull on the north bank of the River Humber in an area called Holderness.[1]

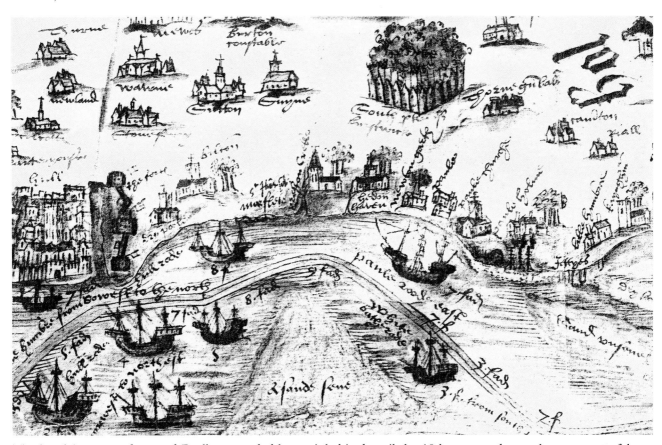

The low-lying ground around Paull was probably not inhabited until the 10th century due to the presence of large areas of salt marsh. A village of 'Pagele' or 'Paghel' is recorded in the Domesday Book as being a berewick (that is a dependent settlement) of the manor of Burstwick; its size was one carucate and it was amongst the land of Drogo de Bevrere. A carucate was a unit of measurement used in the Domesday Book based on how much land eight oxen could plough in a year and, although it could vary slightly depending on location around the country, it equates to approximately 120 acres. This was not the only settlement in the area as Paull Holme and Newton Garth are also listed in the Domesday Book, both also one carucate in size and amongst the land of Drogo de Bevrere.

In the medieval period there were three settlements at Paul. Paull Fleet (later Low Paull) was where the Hedon Haven had its outflow into the Humber. Although the people of Hedon did not hold rights over it – the 2nd charter granted to Hedon by Edward III on 16th April 1348 states: "…they shall not intermeddle themselves in any way with the town of [Paull Fleet] nor with anything arising within the said town of [Paull Fleet] nor with the men of the same in the port of [Paull Fleet]."[2]

Up/over Paull which later became High Paull was the second of these settlements. These two merged sometime in the 16th century to form the present village of Paull, the merger occurring probably because Paull Fleet had been lost to the Humber.

The third settlement was Paull Holme. In the medieval period the coast of South Holderness was being protected by walls "…of which the first recorded are at Paull Holme in 1201…".[3] These walls allowed land to be reclaimed from marsh and converted to farming.

These settlements were treated as being distinct from each other until the 16th century, evidenced by the muster roll accounts which up to 1539 list Paull and Paull Holme separately. The 1539 muster roll for Holderness was taken on "14 April…before Sir Ralph Ellerker, jun., Sir Wm. Constable, and John Wryght." In it Paull and Paull Fleet had to supply 42 men; Paull Holme is listed separately and had to supply nine men. However, after this date there is no separate listing for Paull Holme indicating that there had been a merging of the settlements to form what we now know as Paull. The 1584 Muster Rolls were taken on 22nd September by Sir Christopher Hildyard, John Appleyard and Edward Holme who was a member of the Holme family of Paull Holme. The muster required Paull to supply:

1 corselet
1 bow
1 sheaf of arrows
1 harquebuss (a moveable gun)
1 murrion (a type of helmet usually without a visor)
2 pikemen
9 billmen
4 calevers (a light musket)
4 archers
4 labourers .[4]

The *Victoria County History* states that there were 140 poll tax payers at Paull Fleet, 28 at Up Paull and 61 at Paull Holme in 1377 and that the 1672 hearth tax returns showed 48 households in Paull.[5] In 1811 the population was 574 and in 1901 it was 575. The 1991 census gives the population as 819, and the 2001 census as 765.[6]

What's in a name?

Paull has been referred to as Paghill, Pagele or Paghel and there are two interpretations of the name of Paull. Smith[7] believes it means 'stake' so possibly 'boundary stake'. This is itself maybe based on the Old English words pagol meaning a small peg or pegel meaning a little knob. However, Nicholson[8] believes it is derived from the Celtic word 'pol' or 'pul' meaning miry place, pond or pool. This latter interpretation fits well with the area having been salt marsh prior to the 10th century.

Paull Main Street, *c.*1910

References – Chapter 1

[1] This illustration is a section of a larger map and has a description written by Peck with it. The map is in the collections of the Hull Local Studies Library at the Hull History Centre.

[2] Eds. Gairdner, James and Bordie, *R.H. Letters and Papers Foreign and Domestic, of the Reign of Henry VIII.* Vol. XIV, Part 1, 1894, p. 309.

[3] English, Barbara. *The Lords of Holderness 1086-1260: A Study in Feudal Society.* Oxford University Press, 1979, pp. 203-4.

[4] Brooks, F.W. (ed.) *The Yorkshire Archaeological Society Record Series.* Vol. CXVI, Miscellanea Vol. V, 1951, p. 94.

[5] *The Victoria History of the Counties of England: a History of Yorkshire East Riding Vol. V, Holderness: Southern Part.* Oxford University Press, 1984, p. 114.

[6] Figure taken from www.statistics.gov.uk

[7] Smith, A.H. *Place-Names of the East Riding Of Yorkshire and York.* Cambridge, 1937, p. 36-37.

[8] Nicholson, John. *Place-Names of the East Riding of Yorkshire.* Hull, 1926, p. 84.

CHAPTER 2: HOUSES OF SIGNIFICANCE

Paull Holme

On a minor road in Holderness, running between the villages of Paull and Thorngumbald, stands a lonely tower. Exposed to the elements and the ravages of nature for over 160 years, it is now crumbling and decaying. A grade I listed building, it has been placed on English Heritage's buildings at risk register. Known today as Paull Holme Tower, its origins and interpretation have been the subject of debate amongst historians and archaeologists for centuries. A short article in the *Hull Daily Mail*[9] postulates that the tower is a complete house in itself because it contains service, living and sleeping quarters on three separate levels, suggesting that Paull Holme Tower is a pele tower. However, historic, geographical, archaeological and architectural evidence indicates that the tower is not an isolated structure, disproving this suggestion. In order to offer a more conclusive interpretation of the tower's origins and purpose what follows is an examination of this evidence.

Paull Holme Tower

The tower stands 35 feet high and is made of brick apart from some stone dressings above the windows. The bricks are laid in the English Bond style (alternate rows of stretchers and headers) in alternate courses of brown and blue/grey for decorative effect.

It has three floors:

Basement: at ground floor level, it has a barrel brick vaulted roof. This was probably the servants' area. There is a fireplace in the north wall and at the south end is a staircase providing access to the rest of the tower.

First floor: just one large room with a fireplace and garderobe (a medieval toilet which often discharged straight into a moat) chamber at the northeast corner, both still discernible. In the medieval period moats contained fish as a food source for the occupants of the house and fish would eat the waste from the garderobe. In addition to this, the word garderobe is derived from the same word as wardrobe and people would often hang their clothes near the garderobe to keep moths and flies off them as the insects would find other attractions in the area. There is also evidence of a Tudor arched doorway at the east end of the south wall, but this has been altered at some point.

Second Floor: another fireplace. There have been three two light windows in the north, south and west walls (two of these are now blocked up).

Parapet level: A narrow staircase leads to the once crenellated parapet roof with a wall walk all the way around it. These crenellations suggest that the tower was fortified and so could be said to add to the claim that it is a pele tower. However, these fortifications may have been more decorative than defensive as they only reach waist height.

Paull Holme Tower garderobe.

Also discernible in the walls of the tower is a portcullis slot (right & below) which again suggests this was some sort of fortified manor house. However, the portcullis would not have been the high, wide, large type found in medieval castles and it's perhaps more accurate to call it a yett. Yetts were sturdy gates, which have been described as the "poor man's portcullis"[10] and therefore more a defence against burglary than a fortification.

Early 19th century plans (opposite) of the tower show an 'H' shaped outline in the ground adjoining it which suggests that this surviving tower is only the north wing of a once grand house. Earthworks to the south of the extant tower show the location of the second tower and earthworks between them also indicate the range of the house. This tower was possibly added to an already existing medieval timber-framed building; on the tower's south wall the roof line of the range of the house can still be seen.

Brickwork at Paull Holme Tower.

Varyingly spelt pele, peel and piel (the word means stronghold), a pele tower is a fortified tower house. Peles are commonly found in Northumberland, the Scottish Borders, Cumbria, Wales and Ireland. "There was no question of building halls – for both sides, towers were the only option."[11] Pele towers were easily defended. The entrance doorway would be at first floor level with a retractable ladder or staircase. This would then create a ground floor cellar or basement area for storing valuable goods and even animals. Peles would have thick walls, heavy doors and even portcullises to provide protection. Should a marauder be able to break in to one level, the occupiers could climb higher into their home and seal off each level. The finest extant example of a pele tower is a very grand version at Preston in Northumberland, built in 1392 by Sir Robert Harbottle.

Hussey Tower.

Pele towers like Preston (opposite) were in use between the 14th and 17th century. Paull Holme Tower was built in this period, but as Holderness was not an area of disputes and conflict it is not a pele tower. It's more likely that the tower was added to an existing house as a solar tower with a room or rooms added on to a house to provide more comfortable family living. The 19th century plans also show the moat, which appears on Ordnance Survey maps up to 1927, but is now lost. The 1672 hearth tax returns indicate the size of the house, with its nine hearths. Only three of these are in the tower itself – further evidence that the tower is only part of a larger house. Paull Holme Tower bears many similarities to Hussey Tower in Boston, Lincolnshire and Rochford Tower in nearby Fishtoft.

Hussey Tower (above) stands between South End and Skirbeck Road in Boston, Lincolnshire. Like Paull Holme, it is a three storey, square tower built of brick in the English Bond style. The walls are 3ft, 6" thick and the only stone used is in dressings above the windows. The roof has crenellations and a parapet wall walk all the way around it. Each level of the house is reached via a staircase located in an octagonal turret projecting from the northeast corner of the tower, unlike Paull Holme Tower, where the stairs are inside its square walls. The Hussey family came in to possession of the tower in the 16th century and owned it for many centuries after. However, it was built by Richard Benyngton who was a prominent figure in Lincolnshire society in the mid 15th century, when he was the collector of customs for Boston. He ceased to be active in public life after 1460, but lived until 1475. If he was the builder of Hussey Tower, its date is probably pre 1460. Hussey Tower is thought to be the remnants of a larger house. Evidence in its walls suggests a two storey range ran eastwards from it; the south wall of this range would have run continuously with that of the tower. In 1725 a gable was ordered to be built at one end of the property as much of it had been demolished. Which end is not specified, but it is likely to be the east end and it must have been the range that had been demolished. Hussey Tower also had a gatehouse, brewhouse, mill house and stables, further evidence of its larger size. According to Terence Paul Smith, Hussey Tower was a solar block added to the house to provide more comfortable, lighter accommodation with the ground floor level being used as a cellar.[12] Tower houses were the fashionable property of the 15th century and the well-known example is Tattershall Castle (overleaf, above) also in

Lincolnshire (and not far from Boston). Hussey Tower may have been influenced by Tattershall. Started in 1434, its builder, Lord Ralph Cromwell, knew Benyngton as they were justices together and worked on fen drainage together. Benyngton would have known Tattershall and this could have influenced the building of his own tower which is of course a more modest version of Tattershall. The Tattershall tower was a new construction within the grounds of a medieval castle and Cromwell was adding to his existing accommodation providing a warmer, private and more comfortable living space for himself and his family.

Rochford Tower (below) lies two miles east of Hussey Tower at Fishtoft. Also possibly influenced by Tattershall Castle, Rochford has a stair turret, is built of brick, has a crenellated parapet and also once had a range attached to it. It's believed to date from 1450-60.

Tattershall Castle.

Rochford is a four floor square tower, so has one more level than Hussey and Paull Holme. All three of these buildings are built of brick, which is not the material to use if building for defence as it is easy to breach. Paull Holme Tower therefore must have been built as a comfortable residence. The final piece of evidence to suggest that Paull Holme Tower is only part of a grander medieval house is this drawing of it dated 1816/17:

PAUL HOLME HOLDERNESS YORKS.

The sketch is by an unnamed artist who drew dozens of sites in Holderness between 1816 and 1817. It can be seen that the tower has been added to another building – the tower and rest of the house are clearly made of different material, but are joined together. This sketch has probably not been seen since it was drawn nearly 200 years ago and although the artist is unknown the rest of the sketches in his collection (including one of Paull Church) are so accurate that it seems fair to assume that the artist visited the sites.

A comparison between Hussey and Rochford is particularly important for helping to date Paull Holme Tower. The area of Paull Holme is mentioned in the Domesday Book as one soke of a carucate. In 1295 Alexander of Holme bought the manor of Paull Holme and in the 14th century there are references to a house being built on the site. The tower itself provides clues to its original date. The west wall of the tower bears the Holme family coat of arms, which shows Holmes impaling Wastney – a reference to the marriage of John Holme to Elizabeth Wastney in 1429. This same coat of arms also bears the Tudor Rose which must be a reference to the reign of Henry Tudor from 1485 onwards which could possibly mean the crest was added to the tower at a later date from another location, perhaps another part of the house once it became dilapidated.

What is clear is that the Holme family lived in this manor house for many centuries and by 1588 their total estate in the area was 610 acres. A portrait of one generation of the Holme family exists in the Victoria and Albert Museum. Painted in 1628 it depicts Henry Holme (1570-1631) and his wife Dorothy Grimston. The painting (left) is a triptych, the centre panel showing the couple with the Holme family crest. The other two panels depict children who are unidentified. According to the Holme family tree, the couple had seven children, but the date of birth of only one of them is known, that of Christopher Holme in 1612.

During the English Civil War Christopher and his son Henry were Royalists. Christopher moved to York and Henry fought in the Royalist army. Because of this Paull Holme Manor was confiscated. In 1646 Christopher was petitioning to get the property back and it is stated that: "...he hath had a great part of his houses pulled down and hath had goods and other personal estate taken from him...".[13] The petition appears to have been successful as Henry Holme died there in 1678 (Christopher had died in 1657). What happened to the estate immediately after his death isn't clear, but in 1715 the Rev. Henry Holme (who was living in York) and his son Stephen sold the estate to their cousin John Holme of Skeffling. By this period, according to an entry in the *East Riding Registry of Deeds*, the manor was occupied by a tenant farmer, Thomas Hutchinson.[14] The Skeffling branch of the Holme family were well-established there and can be traced back over many centuries, as the many monuments in the church to them testify. The Skeffling Holmes already had an estate with a moated manor house in the village (now Manor Farm, which appears to have been rebuilt in the early 19th century) so did not take up residency in Paull Holme, which continued to be rented out. John Holme died around 1745 and the estate passed to his two sons the Rev. John Holme, who died in 1775 and Henry Holme who died in 1778. It was through the will of Henry that, in 1811 following the death of his sister Dinah, the estate passed to the Rev. Nicholas Torre, the grandson of Stephen Holme. Members of the Torre family often took on the name of Holme and from 1834 this became their family name. Once again they do not seem to have taken up residency in Paull Holme; according to the 1835 *East Riding Register of Electors* the then owner, James Henry Holme, was resident in Guildford, Surrey. The property is described as a freehold farm and was rented by Benjamin Iveson who, in 1837, had a new house built to the south east using material from the old one, but one tower remained standing, which was restored in 1871 by Colonel Bryan Holme and used as a gazebo. Writing in 1911 Miles and Richardson described it as being in good repair.[15] The picture below is Paull Holme Tower *circa* 1910 and shows the tower in remarkably good condition with its crenellations. In the 1920s the Paull Sand and Gravel Company bought part of the estate and began quarrying there. In the terms of the sale it was stated that they must not obstruct the nearby water course, the moat, indicating that even at this late stage it still had some water in it. The estate was sold to Herbert Johnson in two separate sales of 1921 and 1927. In the first Johnson bought 342 acres from Charles Henry Holme of Rathburne Duns; in the second sale he bought 30 acres from the Paull Sand and Gravel Company.[16] Johnson was still in residence there in 1947 but seems to have been no longer living at Paull Holme in 1951. By this time it was occupied by the Charlton family, although the beneficiaries of Johnson's will still owned most of Paull Holme in 1981. From at least the mid 1980s it has been occupied by the Chapman family.

According to the *Hull Daily Mail* of 21st August, 1947 about a hundred years before "...a large bull managed to find its way in to the abandoned tower and squeeze itself up the narrow staircase to the roof. Unfortunately this bull took one step too many on the roof and fell from it to its death."

The name Paull Holme is of Scandinavian origin meaning a high well-drained site.[17] The area around the tower is on higher ground and this would fit in with the low lying areas around Paull being salt marsh. This settlement is first mentioned in 1086. By 1377 there were 61 poll tax payers at Paull Holme including the Holme family. If other members of these households are taken into account then there could have been a population of around 100 here indicating a village in its own right. There are earthworks to the south east of the tower in the form of field boundaries, platforms and property divisions which are typical evidence of deserted villages.

PAULL HOUSE TOWER. PAULL E/YORKS. F

High Paull House

Paull Holme is not the only manor house of significance in the Paull area. Moving closer to the Humber bank, next to Paull Point Battery and now a car park, is the site of another lost house. In 1769 William Constable sold the 372 acre manor of High Paull to Benjamin Blaydes (the younger), the Hull shipbuilder, for £6,700. A house was built on the land and this house became known as High Paull House or Manor (below). In 1800 the estate was settled on his son Hugh and then in turn to his son H.M. Blaydes and then his son C.B. Blaydes. Hugh Blaydes does not appear to have lived in the house. *The Hull Advertiser* of 16th July 1802 carried an advert: "High Paul – to be let. For a term of five years and entered upon immediately The Mansion-House at High Paul." On the ground floor there was a dining room 21 by 18 feet, a study, servants' hall and two kitchens; on the first floor there were five lodging rooms, a dressing room, a large nursery and four servants' rooms. The house also had coach houses, stables and other offices.

By 1849-50 the estate only comprised 205 acres. In 1853 the manor and 123 acres were sold to Anthony Bannister,[18] a businessman and entrepreneur, who was responsible for building the Hull to Withernsea railway and had a vision of turning Withernsea into an attractive spa town. The property he purchased included pleasure lands to the house, gardens, a lodge, an old shipyard and an old battery. It would appear Bannister didn't occupy the house immediately as the deed of sale names William Smithson as the occupier. However, Bannister did not hold on to the estate for long and 95 acres, one rood and two perches, including the house, were sold again to the War Department. *The Hull Advertiser* in August 1856 carried a small piece stating: "Anthony Bannister, Esq…is said to have parted with his estate at High Paull to the Government, for the purpose of erecting suitable river defences at that point."[19] However, the sale was not announced until another small piece appeared in *The Holderness Times* in November 1860 [20] stating that the War Department had confirmed the agreement entered into for the purchase of the property. Bannister didn't vacate the house at this time as *The Holderness Times* for March 2nd 1861 reported: "Major Bannister, of High Paull, gave a magnificent farewell party to nearly 100 of his friends in Holderness last

Wednesday evening. Dancing was kept up…to a late…hour. There was a magnificent supper…".[21] The conveyance of the property to the War Department was registered on 15th April, but the house was not used immediately as according to White's 1867 *Hull and District Directory*, High Paull was the residence of G.W.T. Ward Esq. By 1874 the electoral register lists George Sunhill Mexon as the rated occupier of the house. However, by 1879 the house was being used as a club house and summer resort for the commandant and officers of the 4th East Yorkshire Artillery Volunteers and by 1889 Kelly's directories were listing the house as "…a store house, offices and quarters for the officers of the battery." It was also to make another contribution to defending the coast line of the area. In 1886 a store was added to the house for use by the Humber Section Coast Battalion Royal Engineers Sub Marine Mining division. How long the house continued to be used by the military isn't clear. I have been told that three families (none of them connected to the military) were living in the house in the 1930s. High Paull House still appears on Ordnance Survey maps in the early 1950s and the electoral registers for the same period list people living there until 1953. The house can be seen in a picture in the *Yorkshire Post* dated 12th June 1950 but a photograph published in the *Hull Daily Mail* in March 1956 shows that High Paull House is gone by then.

The military sold off its property at Paull in 27 lots at auction in 1961. The lots were sold to various buyers, one of whom was Hull City Council who bought three lots including the site of High Paull House. The council converted its land to playing fields and a car park, still there today. Hull Council tried to find a tenant for the buildings still on the land, but as no-one was interested these buildings were earmarked for demolition in 1966. Now sadly all that remains of High Paull House is the lodge house (below) at the entrance to the current car park. This lodge house has been occupied by members of the Beadle family since the early 1960s.

Boreas Hill

Just a little further along the Thorngumbald Road from Paull Holme lies Boreas Hill, the site of another "manor" house (below) and this one still stands. The derivation of the name is uncertain: it could originally have been boar house hill; bower house hill (bower meaning dwelling); its derivation could be from the German word *bauer* or the Dutch word *boer*, both of which mean farmer; it could even be from the Scandinavian (of Swedish origin) word *bor* meaning wind, hence windy hill and of course in Greek mythology Boreas is the north wind. Archaeological evidence suggests the area has been inhabited for many centuries. During gas pipe-laying in the early 1990s, pits containing pottery (believed to be Iron Age), worked wood, iron, bone and flint were discovered.

The current house was built *circa* 1723. However, there may have been a medieval house here acting as a buttery, or bower, to the royal chamber Manor of Burstwick. By 1670 the house belonged to the Carvill (or Carvile) family. There are references to Wilfrid Holme, a knight from Burstwick, having a house called Boreas Hill in 1637 and this could be the

same seven hearth house belonging to Henry Carvile mentioned in the 1672 hearth tax returns. Some believe the south front of the house may date back to the reign of Henry VIII, but the twin gables and pantile roof are typical of the Georgian period. The porch was added in 1936 and is made of bricks taken from the George Inn in High Street, Hull. The will of Henry Carvile, who died on 9th February 1723, refers to a manor house at Bowerhouse Hill, but no other details are given so it isn't clear whether this is the house still standing.[22]

Susannah Stovin, the daughter of Francis Carvile, inherited the estate around 1785. On 24th February in the same year Susannah married James Stovin at Hedon. Tragedy seems to have visited this family often and in quick succession according to the *Monumental Inscriptions* [23] for Paull and the death notices in the *Hull Advertiser*. The former has an entry for an inscription inside the church at Paull stating that on 11th October 1791 Frances Eth. Joanna, daughter of James Stovin died in her infancy. James's own death appears on the same inscription; he died on 25th May 1797 at the age of 35; he is described as an M.D. and magistrate for the East Riding of Yorkshire. James left a will and according to it: "…[I] bequeath unto my said wife, Susannah Stovin, all my household furniture, plate china, linen, horses, carriages, cattle and all the farming stock and utensils I may be possessed of at the time of my demise…". It seems that the Stovins were a well-off family as befitted one living at Boreas Hill. His obituary (*Hull Advertiser*, 27th

May 1797), provides further evidence of this wealth and benevolence: "…He was distinguished for universal philanthropy…and his death is lamented wherever his character was known. He maintained and instructed, at his own expence, ten poor children at the village of Paul, and gave to the poor of his neighbourhood pecuniary relief, medicines, and advice, with the greatest liberality." On 24th December 1808 the *Advertiser* contained a notice for the death of his daughter, 21 year old Miss Margaret Susanna Maria Stovin. The following year saw the *Advertiser* of 8th July reporting the death from consumption of his surviving daughter the 20 year old Miss Sarah-Ann Stovin. Within eighteen years Susannah had lost her husband and three daughters, leaving her alone and without a direct heir to the estate. She survived another thirty years, dying on Monday 18th November 1839 at the age of 77. After Susannah's death there was a large sale of items from the estate including: "four milch cows of very superior breed and symmetry, three in calve and one just calved; 50 tons of old and new hay; as well as household effects, e.g. bedsteads, tables, sofas and crockery."[24]

The 300 acre Boreas Hill Estate now passed to Cornelius Stovin, described as a "gent. of Nine Elms, Surrey".[25] The following year Cornelius sold the estate to Marmaduke Prickett of Hull. On his death in 1861, the estate passed to his son George. The Pricketts don't seem to have always lived in the house as between 1849-1853 the house was occupied by Anthony Bannister. According to the 1851 census he had five servants in the house, but in 1853 he purchased High Paull House.

Boreas Hill was being described as the residence of the late Colonel George Prickett in 1889 when its contents were put up for sale at auction. The contents were so numerous (558 lots in total with many of the lots containing several items in each of them) that the sale took place over two days on Wednesday 19th and Thursday 20th June. Amongst the contents were: "Rich cut-glass and costly ornaments, a valuable library of books, oil paintings and engravings, excellent circular-fronted brougham by a first class London builder." The auctioneers, W.N. Lewendon of the Land of Green Ginger Hull, arranged for a special boat to leave Hull Corporation Pier for Paull each morning of the sale. The catalogue [26] lists items for sale in these rooms:

• Wash house. As well as the usual washing items this room included boat hooks and oars, a wire hen coop and croquet netting.

• Kitchen. This included two bird cages, a spittoon, two hair sieves, a cockatoo with stand.

• Butler's pantry which included four framed pictures.

• Servant's hall containing eight rabbit traps, a 71 piece dinner service, an eight-day clock in oak case.

• Three attic rooms. Amongst the items in these rooms were several bird cages and a flock bed with bolster and pillow.

• Seven bedrooms. Some interesting items here in terms of their quality including an antique Spanish mahogany wash stand, a Spanish mahogany wardrobe, sponge bath with two water cans, mahogany night commode, an iron French bedstead, two cases of birds (I am presuming this meant stuffed birds though the catalogue doesn't specify), a foot bath, a hip bath, a sword, two bows with arrows, a large steel engraving entitled *The Triumph of Christianity over Paganism*.

• Back landing – just the linoleum from this room.

• Front landing and staircase including a stuffed bird and case, "Four of Herring's Fox Hunting Scenes, viz. :- 'the Meet,' 'Breaking the Cover,' 'Full Cry,' and the 'The Death'".

• Entrance hall. From here we have a "very valuable oil painting on copper" (no subject of the painting given), "Two small rare oil paintings with figures" (again no subject specified), "Valuable Print - *King Charles*", an oil painting *View of the Tower, Boreas Hill* (this tower must be Paull Holme Tower, see above, which is sometimes mistakenly referred to as being at Boreas Hill), two photographs of Boreas Hill Hall and Paull Church, a stuffed parrot and case, a stuffed cockatoo and case (this makes me wonder if the cockatoo in the kitchen was stuffed too!), dinner gong and stick.

• Breakfast room. Of the 91 lots in this room 76 were books (many of the lots were several volumes of books), but it also included a fishing rod and stool.

• Dining room. Here we find a 76 piece breakfast service in green and white, a 37 piece green and gold Crown Derby dessert service, a 106 piece gold, white, and green Wedgwood dinner service,…, a stuffed owl in case, a stuffed duck in case, a double-barreled gun, horse-hoof snuff box, a Spanish mahogany telescope dining table with four leaves measuring 9ft 6in by 4ft 6in. The glass ware in this room included eighteen engraved port wine glasses, twelve sherry glasses, twenty engraved sherry glasses, seven claret glasses, thirteen hock glasses, eleven engraved liqueur glasses, eleven engraved bowl champagne glasses and thirteen tumbler glasses.

• Drawing room. This room had a lot of china crockery in it as well as a stereoscope with slides and a "Fine-toned cottage pianoforte in walnut case".

• Stable yard/harness room. Here we find, along with that brougham, three hen coops, a dog kennel, an iron gate and a "Dingey on lake".

The size of the dining table and the amount of crockery and glassware implies that Colonel Prickett liked to entertain; he also seems to have been a keen ornithologist. The house itself was sold in 1891 by George's widow to R.J. Hosdell, a relative of Tuke, the map maker who had created the 1768 map of Holderness. At this time the house was valued at £282 and its size was one rood, 24 pecks. The Hosdell family occupied the house until the death of J. Tuke Hosdell in 1958. It was then bought by Horace Maylin Vipan Wright with only eighteen acres of land and this only included part of the *ha-ha* in front of the house.[27] By this time virtually all of that 300 acre estate had been sold off. In 1967 the house changed hands again when it was purchased by Wilfred Airey,[28] the managing director of Hull Steel Radiators who that November also bought .23 acres of land near Boreas Hill – perhaps this is more of the *ha-ha*.[29] Also in that month Airey paid off the £1,765 balance of his mortgage for the property and the proportions of the estate are given:

> House and gardens, 1.129 acres
> Plantation, 2.722 acres
> Pond, .338 acres
> Plantation, .900
> Bungalow including garden and paddock, 2.612 acres
> Grass, 9.708
> Shelter belt, 1.050   .[30]

Airey died in 1984 in a riding accident during a Holderness Hunt meeting. Since 1985 the house has been occupied by the Worship family.

The house as it stands today is a listed building of six bedrooms, has Adam-style fireplaces in the living and dining rooms and a 6" long key weighing half a pound for the back door. The grounds of the house still retain its gazebo, *ha-ha*, 18th century stone summerhouse, formal walks, lawns, woodland walks with trees that are 100 to 200 years old and wilderness areas.

References – Chapter 2

[9] *Hull Daily Mail*, 14th March 1963.

[10] Morris, Marc. *Castle: a History of the Building that Shaped Medieval Britain*. London, 2003, p. 215.

[11] Ibid, p214.

[12] Smith, Terence Paul. "Hussey Tower, Boston: A Late Medieval Tower-House of Brick", *Lincolnshire History and Archaeology*. Vol. 14, 1979, p. 34.

[13] Clay, J.W. *Royalist Composition Papers II in Yorkshire Archaeological Society Record Series*. Vol. 18, 1895, pp. 139-140.

[14] East Riding Registry of Deeds E319 56, 4th January 1715.

[15] Miles, George T. and Richardson, William. *A History of Withernsea: with Notices of other Parishes in South Holderness in the East Riding of the County of York*. Hull, 1911, p. 219.

[16] East Riding Registry of Deeds: vol. 227 189 157, 11th January 1921; vol. 352 561 452, 31st August 1927.

[17] Jensen. G.F. *Scandinavian Settlement Names in Yorkshire*. 1972.

[18] East Riding Registry of Deeds: HD 250 301, 4th August 1853.

[19] *The Hull Advertiser*, 16th August 1856, p. 6.

[20] *The Holderness Times*, November 1860 (from a collection of newscuttings in Hedon Museum. No exact date or page numbers given).

[21] *The Holderness Times*, 2nd March 1861 (from a collection of newscuttings in Hedon Museum. No page numbers given).

[22] East Riding Registry of Deeds: K 10 11, 1723.

[23] East Yorkshire Family History Society. *Paull Monumental Inscriptions*.

[24] Auction Sale Notice, 26th December 1840.

[25] East Riding Registry of Deeds: FN 243 242, 3rd July 1840.

[26] It is held by the Hull Local Studies Library at the Hull History Centre.

[27] East Riding Registry of Deeds: vol. 1094 12 12, 12th February 1958.

[28] East Riding Registry of Deeds: vol. 1529 31 28, 2nd November 1967.

[29] East Riding Registry of Deeds: vol. 1529 32 29, 2nd November 1967.

[30] East Riding Registry of Deeds: vol. 1529 366 334, 17th November 1967.

CHAPTER 3: IN DEFENCE OF THE REALM, PAULL'S CONTRIBUTION TO PROTECTING THE BRITISH COASTLINE

"The British Isles have always been a standing invitation
to an invader. The long coastline, indented with inlets
and creeks, offers a host of possible landing places,
and it is remarkable that so few attempts to exploit the
possibilities are recorded." [31]

Invasions of the British Isles may have been few, but there have been times when Britain has felt nervous enough about the possibility of invasion to take action to prevent it. This of course means defending the coastline. However, coastal defences are not only about repelling invasion. Britain as an island has a number of ports which are essential to its survival in getting supplies into the country and in times of war ports become prime targets for enemy attacks. The region along the Humber Estuary was no exception to this as Hull was ranked as "the third port and the ninth city of the British Isles" [32] and so the village of Paull had an important role to play.

Early Defences at Paull

Early defences which warned of a threatened invasion were beacons and:

> "Before the reign of Edward III, the beacons were but
> stacks of wood set up on high places, which were
> fired when the coming of enemies was descried; but in
> his reign, pitch-boxes, as now they be, were, instead
> of these stacks, set up; and this properly is a beacon."[33]

However, beacons were also used as navigational aids to shipping, a precursor of lighthouses. Both navigational and defensive beacons were paid for by a tax called beaconage levied by the sheriff. A beacon was sited at Paull and on 30th May 1542 Michael Stanhope (the King's lieutenant in Hull) wrote to the Lord Privy Seal asking "To know upon what occasion the beacon by the bulwark at Pawle 'shalbe set on fire…".[34] In 1588, with the threat of a Spanish invasion, Elizabeth I asked about the state of beacons in the country. Along the banks of the Humber there were beacons at Welwick, Patrington, Boreas Hill, Paull, Marfleet and further west at Hunsley. Naturally these beacons were placed on the highest ground in the area so that they could be seen from long distances. The beacon at Boreas Hill stood in the south-east corner of Beacon Field and in 1887 Nicholson observed that although it had been one of the last in the district it was now gone.[35] Paull was again a beacon site during the Napoleonic Wars when there was a threat of invasion from France. In fact it was such a good early warning system that the beacon system remained much the same as it had ben prior to 1802. Nicholson states that the beacon at Paull was on the clifftop close to the Humber which, by the time he was writing, had been washed away and the beacon:

> "…consisted of a short thick mast, with crosstrees, on
> which stood two tar-barrels, one on each side, close
> to the mast. Affixed to the mast, was a top-mast, which
> displayed a flag…From this it appears that the flag
> would be used during the day, and at night the barrels
> would be ignited."[36]

The picture on the right is taken from the *Hull Times* of 30th May 1914 and is supposed to be a sketch of the Paull beacon as it looked in 1810.

Beacons were a very effective form of early defence and were used from the 14th to the 19th centuries especially during the conflict with Spain in the 16th century and the war with Napoleon in the early 19th century. In the relatively flat Holderness landscape distinctive features such as high ground or coastal edges were essential for the siting of beacons. However, beacons were not the only form of defence, nor were they the only form of defence sited at Paull.

Paull Point Battery

Origins

Paull was not the only place along the Humber to have defences. In 1321 a crenellated wall was built at Hull and in 1530 Henry VIII was worried about a possible war with both France and Spain and so began a series of coastal fortifications. In 1541 he visited Hull and ordered new defences to be built, the result being two blockhouses joined by a curtain wall at the centre of which was a large defensive work known as Hull Castle. Paull as a strategic defensive point also seems to have been recognised in Henry VIII's coastal defence plans because: "Rising ground south-east of Paull village was an apt site for defensive works. In 1542 a battery for twelve gunners was built at Paull."[37] Again, in the same letter as above, Michael Stanhope asks the Lord Privy Seal: "The King appointed a master gunner to have the oversight…at Pawle. Are his wages to continue? And also those of the rest of the gunners? An overseer seems necessary; and he says there may not be less than twelve gunners." (Sic.)

Exactly 100 years later Paull was again used for military purposes. Having been refused entry to Hull, Charles I inspected his troops at Paull in 1642. In addition to this, an earthen battery was built at Paull by the royalist forces in an attempt to stop supplies reaching parliamentarian Hull via the Humber. However, this battery had a short life; only a few months after it was built it was bombarded in to surrender by the parliamentary ships *Lion* and *Employment*.

These two incarnations of the defences show the dual purpose Paull could be put to. Henry VIII saw that Paull could help to defend the River Humber and so the port of Hull, the defences at Paull complementing those at Hull. In the 17th century Charles I saw that Paull could be used as a base to attack Hull and weaken the parliamentarian forces opposing him.

The Napoleonic Wars and the 19th Century

The conflict this time was with Napoleon Bonaparte and France. Following the Peace of Utrecht in 1713, British coastal defences were scaled down and the cannons at Hull were reduced from 117 to 50. By the time of the war with France, coastal defences were inadequate against attack and/or invasion. The defences at Hull were increased and in 1807 an earthen battery was again erected at Paull to hold six 24-pounder cannons (the 1812 map of Paull below shows this Napoleonic battery).

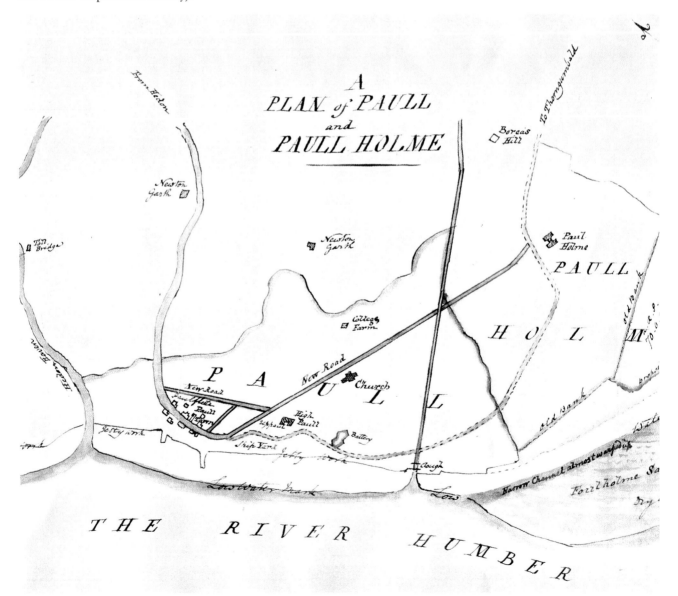

It would appear that this land was summarily taken by the army to build the battery and the owners were not happy. They pursued a compensation claim as evidenced by a series of letters between January and April 1807. A meeting was held on 15th April 1807 at the Humber Tavern in Paull to hear testimony from the owners of the land as to its value. As a result of this meeting the following compensation was paid:

[38]

To be paid to:	£	s	d
Hugh Blaydes Esq.	160	0	0
St. John's College	43	15	0
Mr. Brough	14	17	6
Mr. Roger Blunt	9	12	6
Mr. Hurd	11	16	3
Total	240	1	3
Tenants 3 years	15	17	6
Total	255	18	9

However, these were not the only defences along the Humber; there were also sites at Stallingborough in Lincolnshire and at Spurn Point where there was also a barracks and signal station. According to Dorman the defensive work at Paull was "…known as Paull Cliff Battery, which has disappeared without trace."[39] However, an article appeared in the *Hull Rockingham* on the 20th November 1819 which provides details of the size of the battery:

> "By Order of the Board of Ordinance FREEHOLD ESTATES. TO BE SOLD BY AUCTION, By WILLIAM PEARCE On the Premises, on Wednesday, December, 1819 at Twelve. THREE Acres, more or less, of very excellent GRASS LAND, situated on the CLIFF at PAUL, and lately occupied by the Government as a Battery. Also, the different BUILDINGS thereon; consisting of Barracks for 42 Men, Officers Rooms, Magazines, Materials comprising the Gateway, a Leaden Pump, 60 Large Curb Stones, a quantity of Cheveaux de Frize fit for Fencing. The Materials will be put up in separate Lots. A Plan of the Estate may be seen by applying to the Auctioneers."

There was a long period of peace following the Napoleonic Wars. However, there were significant events happening in the 19th century that were to affect coastal defences and Paull in particular. Next to Paull Cliff and its battery was the estate of High Paull which in 1861 was purchased by the War Department. The department did not make use of the house immediately but by 1879 the house was being used as a club house and summer resort for the commandant and officers of the 4th East Yorkshire Artillery Volunteers; and by 1889 Kelly's directories were listing the house as a store house, offices and quarters for the officers of the battery.

Submarine Miners at Paull

In 1886 a store was added to the house for use by the Humber Section Coast Battalion Royal Engineers Submarine Mining division. Underwater mines (known at the time as torpedoes) were first used successfully in the American Civil War, sinking 57 vessels. This led other nations to assess their use and in 1870 British defence officials recommended supplementing coastal batteries with underwater (in other words submarine) minefields. In 1871, the Submarine Mining Service of the Royal Engineers was formed at Chatham. By 1880 it was recommended that submarine mining corps be formed on the Humber, Tyne, Forth, Clyde, Mersey and Falmouth rivers. However, it wasn't until 1886 that a Hull volunteer corps of submarine miners was formed under the auspices of Sir A.K. Rollit, their service name was the Humber Volunteer Division of Submarine Miners R.E. As it paid more than any other volunteer force, recruitment for the new division was brisk and a company of 60 men was soon formed.

One such recruit was William Henry Willatt, a trainee engineer at Earle's Shipbuilding and Engineering Company in Hull. Willatt's own memoirs[40] provide some details about the submarine miners on the Humber stating that these volunteer units were formed because of possible conflict with Russia. He lied about his age, adding a few months to it to make him eighteen, in order to become its sergeant and: "Most of the engineering students at Earle's Works…joined up." Willatt was sent for two months training to the School of Submarine Mining R.E. at Chatham and again he states that many of the 36 trainees there were from Earle's. At Chatham they were taught to row twelve-oared cutter boats, knotting, splicing, electrical jointing, how to lay mines and flag signalling. The headquarters of the Humber submarine miners were, along with other volunteer corps, at the barracks in Park Street, Hull. However, they would train for and carry out their minelaying duties at Paull and Willatt's memoirs also tell us that regular Submarine

Mining R.E. staff were based at Paull. High Paull House was extended and added to in order to take their technical equipment. The cost of these additions was £5,409; in 1887 a 376 ft pier was added at a further cost of £4,877. This pier held a light railway to carry the mines from the depot to the boats which would take them out in to the Humber. Once laid, cables ran from the mines to the shore and they were detonated electrically from there. In the far right of the picture (above, opposite) the roof line of High Paull House can be seen, along with the buildings added for the Submarine Miners. The start of the pier can also just be seen.

Willatt and his fellow submarine miners at Paull would have used a Thomson Reflecting Galvanometer and a Wheatstone Bridge to maintain these cables. The former was developed in the laying of transatlantic telegraph cables

INSULATING PLUGS.

Plate XXXVI.

HYDRAULIC TESTING.— CONTINUITY TEST.

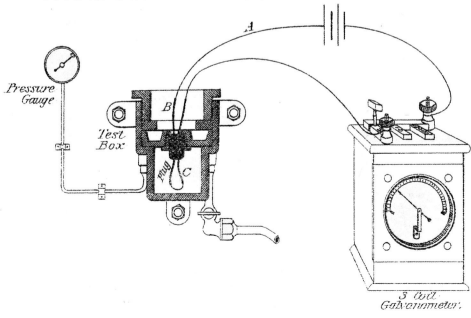

Plate XVIII

CONNECTING UP MINES.
E.C. MINE - FORK SYSTEM.

CONNECTED UP ON TRUCK READY TO RUN TO PIER.

TO PIER.

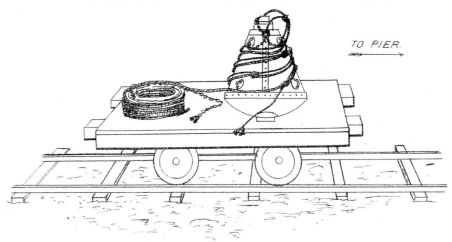

as a means of pinpointing breaks in the cable which could then be repaired. The galvanometers were used by the Submarine Miners at Paull to maintain the cables and keep them in working order. At Paull Point Battery a small observation cell was built in the north-west rampart from which the miners would keep watch and detonate the mines.

The work of the miners required skill and precision as the mines needed to be protected from the fire of coastal batteries and the men would also need a good knowledge of the Humber tides. The *Hull Times* for 11th August 1888 carried a brief account of one of their training camps at Paull. During the week long camp the men took part in drill parade, minelaying practice, making knots, rowing practice, boat racing and athletic competitions. The camp seems to have been, at least partly, a spectator sport as the account states: "Monday being Bank Holiday large numbers of visitors arrived in Paull by boats, which left the Corporation Pier nearly every hour during the afternoon."

Submarine mining proved to be so popular that soon three local companies were formed. However, in 1892, the submarine miners were surprisingly converted into a militia unit. On 1st July 1905 the submarine mining corps in the Humber, Tyne, Tees and Mersey became the 16th Fortress Company and in 1907 volunteer mining corps were disbanded as their role had been taken on by the navy.

The use of High Paull House for military purposes shows that it was not only the fields and purpose-built military installations that were being used in Paull to help defend Britain; any building in the village could be put to use to help defend the Humber and its ports. In addition to this the War Department was adding new housing to the village for its military personnel. A row of houses along the Humber foreshore, now known as Anson Villas, were originally built as the married quarters for the men at the battery and two houses along the access road to High Paull House (now the road to the foreshore car park) were built as accommodation for the officers.

In 1859 the rifled breech loading gun was invented. Compared to the smooth bore muzzle loading guns which fired spherical bullets, the new invention had a greater range and accuracy as well as more penetrating power with its cylindrical shell. There was also the threat of war with France again; this time the antagonism was spearheaded by Napoleon III. Reporting in 1860 a Royal Commission said that the UK's coastline was too long to be defended effectively, but naval bases should be defended and mercantile ports should receive some protection. A new battery at Stallingborough was already under construction in 1859 when the commission was appointed, however this was considered insufficient and a new more powerful battery at Paull was ordered. The new battery was completed in 1864 and "throughout its service life was always referred to as Paull Point Battery."[41] The new battery was an irregular pentagon, its largest side measuring 600 feet running parallel to the Humber; its two other largest sides measured 300 feet each. All the sides were earthen ramparts made from the twelve feet deep ditch dug around the battery. The ditch was flanked in the south-west corners by two-storeyed caponiers which "…have each a casement, from which the ditch may be swept with shell or grape, whilst above the gun is a gallery affording a position for musketry."[42] At the centre of the battery was a bastion which on its extreme ends had two demi-caponiers. On the rear wall were the living quarters, cook house, stores and battery entrance secured by steel gates. The whole battery was surrounded by an unclimbable steel fence. It was armed with nineteen 64-pounder rifled muzzle loader guns housed in brick-lined embrasures above the south and west faces. The gun magazines were stored below where they could be protected by the earthen ramparts.

The battery is not shown on any Ordnance Survey maps until the 1952 revision of map sheet 241 SW, scale 6" to the mile (overleaf) presumably for security reasons. However, security does not seem to have prevented the contemporary writer Sheahan giving a full description of the new battery and its armaments:

"The outer works consist of a sea wall protected by stockades, and a glacis and dry ditch, within which is a loop-holed wall. Behind the wall is a covered way, five feet above the level of the ditch itself; and again, in the rear of this, is the parapet, with its merlons and ramparts all skillfully revetted with sods…at each angle the ditch is protected by caponiers, which give flank fire on the ditch itself, and communicate with the covered way. The caponiers have each a casement, from which the ditch may be swept with shell or grape, whilst above the gun is a gallery affording a position for musketry. The artillery stores and expense magazines are upon the ramparts. The two main magazines are on the parade. Each of the latter is adapted for 400 barrels of powder; and, including the expense magazines, there is accommodation in the fort for 1,200 barrels. In each magazine is a shell-firing room communicating with the power store by a turn-table in the wall…The entrance to the battery is in the rear, through the loop-holed wall, and along this wall are the various buildings required for the troops, viz., barracks, hospital etc."[43]

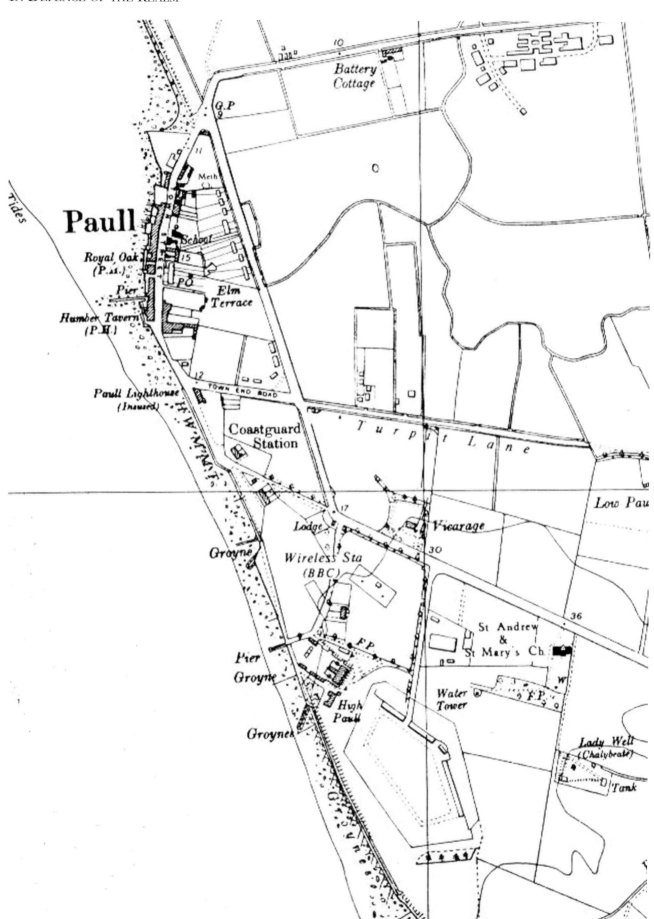

Another source that seems not to have been affected by security concerns is the contemporary directories. Kelly's 1872 directory states "Paull Point Battery, Lieutenant George Leeds, commanding officer; number of men 19; Coast Brigade, Royal Artillery, number of guns 19."[44] The directory gives away the most important strategical information about the battery, that is the number of men and guns. However, one wonders how effective the battery would have been as, in his memoirs Willatt gives the following account of it: "…the guns of the old Battery…were muzzle loaders similar to those used at Trafalgar by Nelson, further and moreover the Battery was so constructed that most of the guns pointed towards Hull, instead of towards the mouth of the River Humber; it was rumoured, that in the time long before, when the Battery was being made, that the War Office had sent the wrong tracing of the plan, or else that the tracing was reversed by mistake…".[45]

According to Saunders "Very early in 1859, Volunteer Corps were being formed in various parts of the country, owing to the unrest then prevailing…".[46] The unrest, although Saunders doesn't say so, must have been the anticipated war with France. On 25th October 1859 the magistrates of the East Riding of Yorkshire held a meeting in Hull to discuss coastal defences and artillery forces. It is possibly from this meeting that the 4th Hull (Yorkshire East Riding) Artillery Volunteers were formed. There were already three other volunteer forces in existence: the 1st were at Burlington (Bridlington); the 2nd at Filey and the 3rd at Hull. The 3rd Hull volunteer force was not a success and ceased to exist in 1860. In August 1880 Burlington and Filey were merged to form the 1st East Riding of Yorkshire Artillery Volunteers and the 4th Hull became the 2nd East Riding of Yorkshire Artillery Volunteers. In 1902 the name changed again, this time to the 2nd East Riding of Yorkshire Royal Garrison Artillery (Volunteers) or the 2nd E.R.Y.R.G.A.V. for short. During times of war these volunteer artillery corps would man coastal defences and for the 2nd E.R.Y.R.G.A.V. this included Paull Point Battery. The headquarters of the 2nd E.R.Y.R.G.A.V. were in Park Street, Hull where they met every week for drill and gun training. Training at coastal batteries was usually undertaken at annual camps which were often held at Paull.

In the 1881 census there are 42 people listed at the battery. There are only nine single men, the other 33 people being made up of eight families. In total there are seventeen men manning the battery, the rest being family members. Of the 42 people only one was born locally, Mary McGlone at Paull itself, the one year old daughter of Robert McGlone corporal of the battery. All the other people at the battery are from outside the area with sixteen giving their birthplace as Ireland. The seventeen men manning the battery all give their occupation as Gunner Royal Artillery. They must have been there for at least a year as Mary McGlone is one year old and born at Paull. The census returns for Paull in other years usually show artillery men and royal engineers with their families at the battery, with the vast majority of the people listed not local. In times of peace the battery was probably manned by regular units of artillery then at times of war these regular units would be transferred to the front and the volunteer corps would take over.

Coastal defences were again reviewed in 1887 by a committee led by Edward Stanhope, the Secretary of War, the review was needed because of a new design of rifled muzzle loading guns in the form of 6 inch breech loading guns. Paull Point Battery's rifled muzzle loader guns were replaced with two 9.2 inch and four 6 inch breech loading guns as well as four rifle muzzle loading guns. In 1894 the battery had to be remodeled to take the new breech loading guns which were now housed in concrete barbette emplacements below with hand operated hoists. It was also at this time that Paull received three Defence Electric Lights (DEL), a new type of searchlight that was to prove useful later on. The battery may have been altered to house new guns, but it seems the men who served there in 1896 were suffering: "Married men are allowed to live away from the battery, as there is no convenience for them inside. Apart from this, the battery has been declared unsanitary…the single men had been ordered out, and were living in tents on the adjoining ground. Hundreds and hundreds of pounds have been spent in the attempt to improve the drainage of the battery, but up to the present such attempts have been unsuccessful."[47]

For Paull Point Battery the 19th century ended as it had begun, with the battery in a state of readiness to repel invasion or attack. Changes had been made to the way it was manned, to its building fabric and to its armaments in order to maintain this readiness. The challenges to come in the 20th century would not find Paull Point Battery wanting.

The 20th Century and Two World Wars

The first decade of the 20th century once again saw Paull being used for training by the 2nd E.R.Y.R.G.A.V. *The Hull Gunner*, the weekly newspaper of the volunteer force often carried an account of these training sessions and even pictures of the men training. The issue of 12th July 1902 describes a typical day of the camp on Monday 7th July: "Very soon marching drill in ducks (white ones), signaling practice, fatigues &c., were on the way. After breakfast (and everyone seemed ready for it) gun practice took place…". This was a week long camp and the account continued in the following week's newspaper, which even provided a plan of the encampment (opposite). The 2nd E.R.Y.R.G.A.V. were back at Paull in August 1903: "…and in the coming week the seagulls will be disturbed by the unwonted firing of heavy guns, and the village will be over run with thousands of people. Large crowds of visitors came over to Paull during the day and evening, and the field, after tea, was a scene of great animation."[48]

Sunday service at Paull camp.

The Hull Gunner only ran between 1901 and 1904 and so the next account of a camp at Paull appeared in 1907 in *The Hull and East Riding Graphic*. According to this the purpose of the camp was "…to repel an attack of the enemy landing in small boats…[and]…Then followed the main object of the mobilization scheme, the manning of the guns at night."[49]

Paull Point Battery wasn't just being used by local volunteer forces. In February 1903 extra bedding was arriving at the battery and "…fifty extra artillery men are daily expected to take up their quarters here."[50] On 27th June 1903 the *East Yorkshire Telegraph* was reporting the arrival of the Durham Royal Garrison Artillery Volunteers at Paull.[51]

In 1905 there was another review of coastal defences, this time undertaken by the Committee of Armaments for Home Ports. It believed the existing defences at Paull Point Battery were good enough to deal with a class C attack which would be from an unarmoured vessel and no plans for further defences at the battery were made. In 1911, the new docks at Immingham and Marfleet and a naval oil store at Killingholme brought another review of the Humber defences. The existing guns at Paull were considered insufficient to protect the new constructions, so it recommended that new batteries should be built downstream. Spurn Head was rejected because of the instability of the ground so sites at Stallingborough and Sunk Island were chosen. Paull's importance in defending the Humber was diminishing.

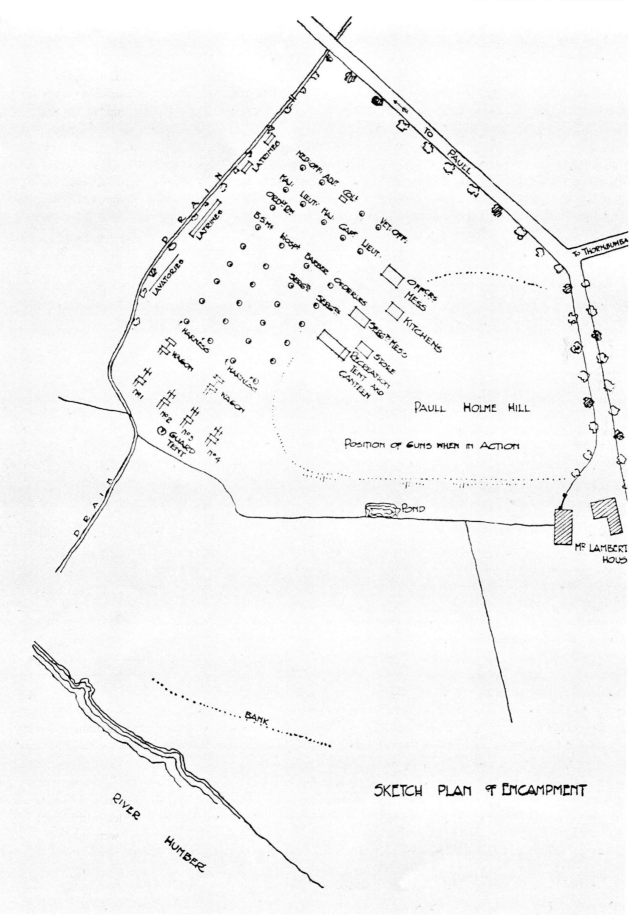

SKETCH PLAN OF ENCAMPMENT

By 1913 there was the threat of war with Germany, particularly significant because it threatened North Sea trade and ports. However, when war finally broke out in 1914: "Unfortunately Paull Point Battery was still the only means of viable defence, but with the impetus of war, work on the new batteries at Stallingborough and Sunk Island was pushed ahead with all speed."[52] By November 1914, a War Office memo stated that Paull Point Battery was to be dismantled when the guns at Stallingborough and Sunk Island became operational, but the battery was to remain the headquarters for the Humber defences throughout the war. By early 1915 Stallingborough and Sunk Island were partially operational and the latter was also to have a role in supporting the examination service which had to identify the character and intent of vessels wishing to enter the Humber ports and for this purpose a port war signal station was erected at Sunk Island. William Henry Willatt, who was one of the first volunteers of the Submarine Miners based at Paull, worked on the construction of Sunk Island Battery, particularly with the electrical generating equipment and the search light projectors. The War Emergency Programme was implemented in 1915 and this recommended new batteries at Kilnsea, Spurn Head as well as island forts at Bull and Haile Sands. These new batteries were intended to intercept any raiding or invading forces before they reached the mouth of the Humber. The width of the mouth of the river meant that shore batteries would have difficulty controlling the river at night or in poor visibility; island forts would solve this problem. During 1916 the batteries at Kilnsea (known as Godwin Battery) and those on the Spurn peninsula became operational. Construction difficulties at Bull and Haile Sands forts meant they were not completed until the end of the war in 1918.

The guns at Paull Point Battery had diminished in importance, but other services based there still had a vital role to play in repelling the enemy. In World War I many British towns were suffering from bombing raids by Zeppelin airships. Hull was no exception and suffered quite badly from these raids. However: "…on 25th September 1917, an attempted raid was driven off as the Zeppelin was held by the Paull searchlight, and chased by a fighter plane."[53] The Defence Electric Lights installed at Paull in the 1890s had proved their usefulness and were an impressive sight: "On the foreshore, we noted like two giant's eyes peering out of their specially constructed 'hill', the mammoth electric searchlights which can sweep the Humber and startle the inhabitants on the Lincolnshire side."

Stationed at nearby Boreas Hill was the rarely heard of M Company, 3rd East Yorkshire Regiment. The Company had been formed there on 22nd January 1916 and according to the Snapper (the Journal of the East Yorkshire Regiment): "During the six weeks of its existence the company has received 22 recruits and the same number of home-service men who perform the various duties appertaining to the smooth running of a company."[54] This writer goes on to remark that nothing of importance had happened in the area apart from the excitement caused by a recent Zeppelin raid which seemed to be heading for the camp and: "…one n.c.o. shouted 'Get clear of the buildings!' (quite a compliment to the huts.) In the company of a couple of men he made off in the direction of a clump of trees near by, but was pulled up short by an open drain which had been dug recently close to the huts. When he extricated himself from the drain which was full of snow he was an excellent snowman. Meanwhile the surrounding atmosphere was blue, and his remarks concerning persons who dug drains were very pointed and venomous." (Ibid.)

Immediately after World War I the defences built along the Humber during the war were consolidated and district establishments were set up at Paull and Godwin batteries from which regular gunners could maintain the guns and equipment in their charge. Coastal defence policy was periodically reviewed. However, money seems to have been the watchword and by the early 1930s the armaments at North Killingholme, Stallingborough, Sunk Island and Green (Spurn Head) batteries were withdrawn. It had already been decided in 1926 that coastal defences would be manned by the Territorial Army and the East Riding Heavy Regiment, Royal Artillery (TA) would defend the Humber. They practised at drill halls and annual camps, some of which were held at Bull Sands Fort and Godwin Battery. Around 1934 two 6 inch breech loading guns were removed from Paull Point Battery for use by the local TA gunners.

When war broke out again in 1939, the Humber defences had only eight guns left compared with 22 at the end of World War I. During the winter of 1939-40 the Germans embarked on an extensive mine-laying programme in the Humber. As a result coastal batteries were re-armed. Britain was again worried about invasion when France fell in June 1940 and Germany was occupying the Low Countries. "By the beginning of 1941 the River Humber and its associated ports had become one of the best defended areas in Great Britain."[55] However, Paull Point Battery was not re-armed. It had a secondary role to play in being a storage depot for the ammunition of the Humber anti-aircraft defences and also played a major role in protecting shipping from the magnetic mines developed by the enemy. These mines would be dropped by planes in to water channels, like the Humber. As a ship passed over them its magnetic hull would draw the mine to it and as it attached itself to the ship the mine would explode. Thanks to a stray magnetic mine being found at Shoeburyness British wartime experts were able to develop a counter-measure to these mines which were causing severe losses amongst British naval and merchant shipping. The process was known as "degaussing" and involved wrapping the ship's hull in coiled wire which countered its magnetism so that the mines would not stick. These coils would be fitted at a shipyard, and were activated as the ship entered potential mined areas. Degaussing stations were set up, with one of these operated by Wrens at Paull Point Battery (below, left). From a control tower and lookout point over the Humber the Wrens would examine passing ships to check they had been degaussed and then press a button as they passed over a wire which activated the coils' demagnetizing effects.

Despite this Paull Battery no longer had a direct role to play in defending the Humber and as the end of 1943 approached it seemed that invasion was unlikely and that the number of operational coast defence batteries could be reduced. With the invasion of Europe in 1944 further economies were made and by January 1945 all batteries on the Humber ceased to be operational. Only the guns at Spurn Head and Bull and Haile Sands Forts were maintained. However, areas around Paull were to play another important role in defending Hull against enemy attack.

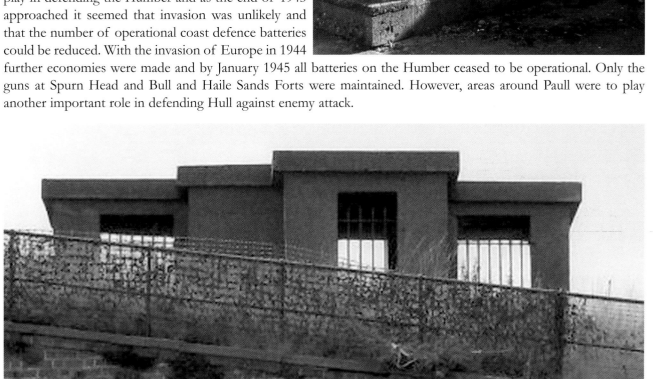

Decoy Sites

In recent years it has come to light that many areas around the country were used as decoy sites during the Second World War in order to fool German bombers and deflect their bombs from the intended target. Areas around Paull were chosen as decoy sites.

The City of Hull was described by the wartime Home Secretary as the worst bombed town or city in Britain. Hull was raided 82 times during the war with more than 1,200 civilians killed, 3,500 houses and 25 schools destroyed, 85,000 houses and 85 schools seriously damaged.[56] This heavy bombardment had to be curtailed and so in March 1941 under the auspices of Colonel Turner's department of the Secret Air Ministry a scheme was devised to create decoy sites. The scheme became operational by August 1941 and land at Thorney Crofts and Little Humber, east of Paull, was chosen to create replicas of Hull's docks. Decoy sites were managed by the Royal Navy and were built at one-third scale.

The decoy sites around Paull used lights to create the outline shapes of towns and docks. Lights were mounted on 10 feet poles (below) and shone down on water held in specially constructed concrete ponds. From high altitude these ponds looked like the docks at Hull with the lights representing the essential dockside lighting. There were three types of ponds all usually with 1.5 foot high concrete walls and a concrete base: rectangular ones usually about 30 feet by 16 feet; right hand triangular ones of about 21 feet by 21 feet used to represent the angles of docks; and a five sided pond of about 30 square feet used to represent the re-entrant angles of the dock. The most easterly decoy site was near Thorney Crofts and consisted of sixteen ponds (most are still visible) used to represent King George V Docks at Hull. Due south of Old Little Humber Farm are eight ponds used to replicate Hull's Alexandra Dock. The narrowness of the shoreline at this point meant that only the northern half of the dock could be imitated. Another narrow shoreline south of Little Humber Farm meant Victoria Dock could only be represented by five ponds (these have partially survived).

Lying south-west of Little Humber farmyard is a cement rendered brick building, with a flat reinforced concrete roof, containing two rooms protected by blastproof walls. This was the decoy sites' control shelter used to operate the lights, which were powered by a diesel generator housed in one of the building's rooms; the other room provided accommodation for the crew and acted as a bomb shelter. These decoy sites had some success in deflecting the German bombers from Hull and contributed to lessening the destruction of the city. Decoy sites were decommissioned on 8th March 1945 and the sites around Paull have been given listed building status.

The End of Coastal Defences

By the early 1950s weapons technology, especially with guided missiles, was so far advanced that on the 17th February 1956 the Minister of Defence announced in the House of Commons that Coast Artillery in the British Army would be abolished on the 31st December. This was the end for Paull Point Battery and by 1961 it was in private hands. It was sold again in 1984 and in 1986 it was scheduled as an Ancient Monument; the battery is now open to the public as a military museum.

References – Chapter 3

[31] Hogg, Ian V. *Coast Defences of England and Wales 1856-1956*. Newton Abbot, 1974, p. 13.

[32] The Ministry of Information. *Roof Over Britain: the Official Story of Britain's Anti-Aircraft Defences 1939-1942.* London, 1943, p. 38.

[33] Nicholson, John, *Beacons of East Yorkshire*. Hull, 1887, p. 1.

[34] Gairdner, James and Brodie, R.H. *Letters and Papers Foreign and Domestic Of the Reign of Henry VIII*. London, 1900, p. 208.

[35] Nicholson, *Beacons of East Yorkshire*. p. 32.

[36] Nicholson, *Beacons of East Yorkshire*. p. 49

[37] Kent, G.H.R. 'Paull', in *The Victoria History of the Counties of England: a History of the County of York, East Riding, vol. v Holderness: Southern Part*. Ed. K.J. Allison. Oxford, 1984, p. 123

[38] Taken from document LT 9/23 held by the East Riding Archives Office, Beverley.

[39] Dorman, Jeffrey E. *Guardians of the Humber: a History of the Humber Defences 1856-1956*. Hull, 1990, p. 45.

[40] Henry Willatt, William. *This Incarnation: being Recollections of William Henry Willatt*. Malet Lambert Local History Originals, vol. 25, 1985, pp. 18-22.

[41] Dorman. *Guardians of the Humber*, p. 45.

[42] Sheahan, James Joseph. *History of the Town and Port of Kingston upon Hull*, 2nd ed. Hull, 1866, p. 354.

[43] Ibid.

[44] Kelly, E.R. (ed.) *The Post Office Directory of the North and East Ridings of Yorkshire with the City of York*. London, 1872, p. 531.

[45] Willatt. *This Incarnation*, p. 21

[46] Saunders, Major R. *History of the 2nd East Riding of Yorkshire Royal Garrison Artillery (Volunteers) Hull*. Hull, 1907, p. 1.

[47] *Hull News Supplement*. Saturday 11th July 1896, p. 11.

[48] *The Hull Gunner*. 8th Aug 1903, p. 3.

[49] "Hull Artillerymen at Paull Point Battery", *The Hull and East Riding Graphic*. 23rd May 1907, pp. 7-9.

[50] *East Yorkshire Telegraph*. 28th February 1903.

[51] *East Yorkshire Telegraph*. 27th June 1903.

[52] Dorman. *Guardians of the Humber*, p. 22.

[53] Kimberly, Stephen. *Humberside in the First World War*. Hull, 1988, pp. 39-40.

[54] *Snapper: the Monthly Journal of the East Yorkshire Regiment*. March 1916, p. 48.

[55] Dorman. *Guardians of the Humber*, p. 30.

[56] Figures taken from: Department for Culture, Media and Sport. Scheduled Entry for World War II Decoys for Hull Docks. London, 2001.

In the early 16th century hills, cliffs, churches and prominent buildings were used as markers to aid navigation; from 1585 buoys and beacons were used. The latter, an early form of lighthouse, provided a guiding light for ships to follow. Paull was an obvious choice to site such aids to navigation.

In December 1647 Trinity House entered into a seven year agreement with "…William Ridsdale, of Paull, boatman, for the maintenance of the beacon called Burkham Beacon, in the Humber. [Trinity House] agreed to provide a pole of fir 30 feet long, which Ridsdale agreed to set up with a cape at his own cost and subsequently to maintain it at his own costs, and to replace it if driven away during the term of seven years."[57] Ridsdale was to be paid 15s upfront for the beacon, 5s at Christmas in the following year and then 20s each Christmas for the remaining years of the agreement. By 1776 a beacon to aid navigation had been erected on the north-west foreshore at Paull. In 1831 Trinity House paid 7s 6d for the whitewashing of a house at Paull as a marker for ships and by 1835 £2 a month was being paid to the keeper of the Humber Tavern for the rent of a room where a lantern was placed as a guide to shipping. However, a more permanent guide was needed and Trinity House decided to build two lighthouses at Paull, although only one was built, at a cost of £60. Completed in 1836 the Paull Lighthouse (below) stands 40 feet tall, was built of brick with a cement coating and was originally painted red. It had a fixed white light with a red sector provided by a red glass in front of each of the three reflectors. The light was provided by a catoptric lantern of three lamps, each of which had its own oil burner. The burner needed 150 gallons of rape oil and 18.5 cotton wicks per year to run it. The first lighthouse-keeper at Paull was James Campbell who lived in the cottage attached to the lighthouse and was paid £55 per annum as well as an allowance of coal and oil.

The continually shifting sand in the Humber off Paull meant that fixed lighthouses were not always a sufficient aid to shipping. In 1868 Trinity House tested movable lights at Thorngumbald Clough further along the front at Paull. The military at Paull Point Battery objected to the idea as it believed the lights would be in the line of their fire and they suggested finding another location or building lights that could be dismantled in times of war. Trinity House insisted that there was no other suitable location and tenders were sought for the lighthouses' foundations. Storey says that originally it had been intended to build a high light at 50 feet, but this was reduced to 40 feet and the second low light at 22 feet.[58] However, in 1939 the Humber Conservancy Board describes the high light as 49 feet and the low light as 32 feet.[59] The low light was on a trolley enabling it to be moved about (for a maximum distance of 26 feet) as required by the conditions in the Humber; the high light was painted red and the low light was painted white. A lighthouse-keeper's cottage (painted red) was also to be built next to the new lights. Storry and Jagger of Hull were employed to build it and the foundations of the lights for £452 5s 2d. The lighthouses (below) themselves were built by Thompson and Stather of Hull at a cost of £1,064 (for four lights, two here at Paull and two at Salt End). These new lighthouses had fixed white lights and became operational in July 1870. By 1872 the original lighthouse in Paull was being used as a telegraph station. The 1836 lighthouse was offered to the War Department for £450, but they declined to take it on.

In 1907 the Humber Conservancy Act was passed and on 1st of January 1908 the newly created Humber Conservancy Board took over the running of navigational aids on the River Humber. By September 1908 it was recommended to the Board that as far as the 1836 lighthouse was concerned "…no other use can be made of it than to let it; for which purpose it would be necessary to expend at least £5 for repair" and it was decided that tenancy offers should be sought.[60] Perhaps tenants were not found as I have been told that the lighthouse could be hired as holiday accommodation around this date; an article on Paull in the *Hull Times* of 1913 says the lighthouse is used as a private dwelling[61] and by 1936 the lighthouse was under repair after storm damage.[62] In 1947 the lighthouse is again referred to as a residence in the Humber Conservancy Board's Annual report which states: "The Board's old lighthouse at Paull, which was used as a residence, became vacant in March, 1947, and the building was sold." for £600 to Mrs. Scales.[63] By 1950 Mrs. Scales wanted to travel and decided to go to Africa; she hoped to rent the lighthouse out whilst away having : "…had practically the whole of the inside rebuilt and modernised."[64] Mrs. Scales had had running water and electricity installed. Almost a year later the lighthouse was up for sale again at auction, but withdrawn when the price reached £1,500 having failed to meet its reserve. A sale later in the decade was more successful and the lighthouse at Paull is still a private residence today. Every owner of the lighthouse (even to this day) has to agree never to show a light at the top of it in case it confuses passing ships.

A 1957 magazine article states there used to be an underground passage running from the lighthouse to the beach. No explanation is given and no other description of the lighthouse mentions it, so it may be a myth.[65]

The two lighthouses at Thorngumbald Clough were operational for over 70 years. In August 1948 it was proposed that the lights (along with those at Salt End) cease operating. This was a sad day for their keeper of 29 years, Henry Curtis, due to retire the following year. He would be allowed to stay on at the cottage if he wished, a cottage with no running water (the Curtis family drank filtered rain water), no electricity, no gas, no wireless and no easy access. Only a narrow path along the foreshore led to it and the oil and coal needed to run the lights and supply the keeper's

A view of Paull Beach. The large building to the right with the flagpole is the coastguard station.

cottage were brought by boat and this would stop once the lights ceased to be operational. Henry's job as lighthouse-keeper was to keep the lights clean, trim their wicks and carry out general maintenance on them. The lights were lit everyday at sunset and put out at sunrise; their beam could be seen five miles away. However, according to the 1952 Humber Conservancy Board annual report: "On 29th November, the Thorngumbald High and Low Lights were re-established."[66] It was not an easy life for a lighthouse-keeper at Paull. One of his predecessors found it also had a financial constraint. In March 1894 Trinity House appointed Thomas Winson as the new keeper of the Thorngumbald Clough lighthouses. Winson at this time was master of the Spurn Lifeboat. In his new post as lighthouse-keeper he would be paid £60 a year but he had to put up a surety of £200 as a guarantee that he would carry out his duties diligently.[67] The now disused lighthouses still stand today. The keeper's cottage has gone.

There is also mention of a coastguard station at Paull in the 19th century, which was rebuilt in 1905 and closed in the early 1920s. The building itself remains and has been converted to houses.

References – Chapter 4

[57] Brooks, F.W. (Ed.). "The First Order Book of the Hull Trinity House 1632 – 1665". *The Yorkshire Archaeological Society Record Series*, Vol. CV for the year 1941.

[58] Storey, Arthur. *Hull Trinity House History of Pilotage and Navigational Aids of the River Humber (1512-1908)*. Trinity House, 1971, pp. 51-3.

[59] Butterfield, A.E. *Humber Conservancy Board: Report on the Lighthouses, Lightships, Light Floats, Buoys and Vessels Belonging to the Board*. January 1939, p. 9.

[60] Taken from the minutes "At a Meeting of the Wrecks, Buoyage and Beaconage Sub-Committee, Held at The Conservancy Offices, Kingston-upon-Hull, on Thursday, the 3rd of September, 1908." p. 398. Held by Hull City Archives.

[61] *The Hull Times*, 23rd August 1913, p. 8.

[62] *The Hull Times*, 29th February 1936, p. 14.

[63] Humber Conservancy Board. *Fortieth Annual Report with Accounts for the Year Ended 31st December 1947*. p. 4.

[64] *Hull Daily Mail*, 11th August 1950.

[65] Wood, Bernard G. "A Lighthouse is their Week-end Dream Home" in: *Yorkshire Life*, January 1957, pp. 31-32.

[66] Humber Conservancy Baord. *Fifty-Fifth Annual Report for the Year Ended 31st December 1952*. p. 4.

[67] "Bond Between Mr. Thomas Winson and the Corporation of the Trinity House Hull", 5th March 1894. Held by Hull City Archives at The Hull History Centre (DPD/1/5/15).

CHAPTER 5: RELIGION
The Parish Church

There has been a church at Paull since 1115 A.D.. Paull Church may have originally been located next to Paull Holme Manor (approximately one mile east of the current church). A nearby field is called "chapel dale" and Robert Holme of Paull Holme Manor, in his will of 1503, states that a mass should be held in Paull Holme Chapel for the life of his wife and 20 years after her death. This chapel was still in existence, but in a poor state of repair, in the reign of Queen Anne. This could have been a private chapel attached to the house. *The Hull Times* of February 1928 reports a "Curios find…upon the land at Paull Holme…"[68] near the remaining tower of Paull Holme Manor. Human skulls and bones along with a horseman's spur were unearthed. The article surmises "…that in feudal times fighting took place on this particular spot and the dead were buried here."[69] However, is it possible that these burials are from the church (if located at Paull Holme) or the chapel referred to in Robert Holme's 1503 will, which would mean that the remains are members of the Holme family. This would also account for the lack of monuments to the family in the Paull parish church. An alternative explanation for these human remains may be due to the English Civil War. The Holme family of the period were royalists, Paull itself was a royalist camp and these remains could be royalist casualties. Unfortunately there doesn't appear to have been any further newspaper articles on these human remains nor does the article that first mentions them say where the skulls were removed to and so their mystery may never be resolved.

A church is also referred to on the bank of the Humber. According to the Patent Rolls for 1355: "Licence…to the rector of the parish church of Paghel in Holderness, of an acre of land in the same town…to construct a parish church and churchyard. The present church, situated on the coast of the water of Humbre, having been almost entirely broken down and inundated the rector and parishioners propose to build a new one."[70] So the present church was built soon after 1355, was dedicated to St. Mary and from the 15th century St. Andrew was used as an alternative or joint dedication, but today it is only known as St. Andrew's.

According to Poulson[71] in his history of Holderness the current church in Paull was built after the restoration of the monarchy in 1660 because the original church had been destroyed in the English Civil War. This opinion seems to be based on an account of the 1643 siege of Hull in Tickell's *History of Hull*.[72] However, this appears to be wrong and a mistake then repeated by other historians writing about Paull. In 1872 the church is described architecturally as "Perpendicular" which would place it at least in the pre-reformation period.[73] Bulmer states that in the restoration

INTERIOR PAULL CHURCH. E.YORKS.

work of 1878 traces of fire were discovered proving that the church had suffered damage during the 1643 siege of Hull, but not destroyed.[74] This opinion was shared by a *Hull Times* reporter in 1913 who stated: "When the parliamentarian ships were in the Humber in 1642…many a stray shot landed at the Parish Church, as there was abundant evidence when restored…but fortunately the church escaped entire demolition."[75] According to Pevsner and Neave: "The tall unbuttressed mid 14th century tower has foiled Y-tracery to the windows of the upper storey…The church was burnt in the siege of Hull in 1643, and repaired in 1663 and 1669."[76] showing that architectural experts seem to agree that the church is at least medieval, some placing it in the 14th century which matches the entry in the Calendar of State Papers mentioned above. The Hull Bench Book for 28th May 1657 carries an appeal to hold a collection in the town for "…the repairing of Paull Church…"; and the bench book for 25th June 1657 states that £20 4s had been collected. The key phrase is "the repairing" of the church and not the building of a new one.[77]

The Rev. Cordeaux, vicar of Paull during its 1870s restoration states that: "…the registers, which were remarkably well kept at this period by John Smithson, the vicar of Pagula, commencing in 1657 (the previous records having, doubtless, been lost) and containing no reference whatever to any removal of the church…[and]…no record of any consecration of the church since the restoration can be found in the archbishop's register."[78] In a follow up letter to *The Hull Times*, the Rev. Cordeaux says: "I have been informed that a quantity of human bones were at one time seen and discovered in the mud on the foreshore, as well as on the cliff adjoining, where the Battery now stands."[79] He goes on to conjecture whether these were buried in an old churchyard of Paull or merely the remains of the sad unfortunates to be washed up on shore and buried on "Paull green". This green is referred to as a burial site for washed up bodies at Paull in the parish registers as early as 1685 (but it no longer exists having being lost to coastal erosion).

Sir Stephen Glynne[80] also describes the church as in a poor state of repair; this despite an article in the *Hull Advertiser* 4th January 1832 stating that: "The Parish Church of Paull, near this town, has been re-opened for divine service, after receiving considerable alteration and improvements."[81] However, major restoration work was again carried out between 1877-9 and, as is often the case with Victorian church restoration work, this may have covered up or even destroyed many of the original medieval features of the church. The church re-opened on Thursday 7th August 1879 and the work, costing a total of £1,600, included repairs to the tower columns, the nave arches, column bases, a new pine pitch roof, re-tiling of the chancel, new glazing and new pews. After the opening ceremony a luncheon was provided at the nearby Paull Point Battery "…which was crowded by a large company of ladies and gentlemen of the surrounding district."(Ibid) Minor repairs were carried out again in 1925 to the falling brickwork in the tower and the walls near to the ceiling which had been crumbling, so they were cemented over to prevent further decay. The heating system was also overhauled and the church given a thorough cleaning. A *Hull Times* reporter writing in 1928 stated the church looked shabby and crumbling from the outside, but the interior was in a very good sate of repair.[82] In 1964 the tower of the church was restored at a cost of £540 as its walls had been eroded to half their 4 feet thickness and it was in danger of collapsing. The parishioners had been saving for the repair since the war.

Decay was not the only problem to be faced by St. Andrew's church. In February 1832 the church suffered a burglary in which "…some villains…carried away a quantity of bibles and testaments, appropriated for the use of the children of the poor."[83] There were also problems with at least one of its curates. *The Hull Advertiser* on the 4th January 1839 reported the "Unbecoming Conduct of a Country Curate."[84] The Rev. J.S. Jones falsified entries on a government form investigating the amount of religious education carried out in the parishes of the country by over-estimating the number of parishioners the Paull church could hold and understating the number of people nearby non-conformist chapels could hold. In addition to this, Jones also used the form to extol his own virtues and criticise his parish employers by saying:

"We have no vicar resident because we have no vicarage house; we have a curate, anxious to reside among us, and perform his duties conscientiously, who in order to obtain residence amongst the parishioners, expends more than his income from the church; but as there is only one house fit for him to live in, we take advantage of his necessity by raising his rent and 'sweating him well'. At Ladyday next, we hope to extort £15 per annum more from him…"

The Rev. Jones did not get away lightly as the author of an *Hull Advertiser* article, who called himself the "Castigator", proceeded to point out his shortcomings by saying: "Before Mr. Jones had been curate of Paull three years [our] large congregation had reduced to about half a dozen persons. The Sunday school, under his management, became extinct…".[85]

The church may have stood the test of time and of war, but the accommodation for the vicar of Paull did not fare so well. A house with six rooms on the ground floor alone for the vicar of Paull is mentioned in 1650. However, in the 16th century and in 1637, the vicar is living at Thorngumbald.[86] In 1743, according to Archbishop Herring's Visitation, the then vicar, William Robson, reported: "I do not reside upon the Cure, there being no Vicarage House, the ground upon which it stood having been swallowed up by the Humber above Forty Years ago, & (as I have been informed) the Materials of it converted by the Late Vicar Mr. James to his own private use."[87] and consequently he lived at Thorngumbald. In the 1850s the vicars of Paull were taking matters into their own hands in getting a vicarage built in the village. An enquiry was made regarding Queen Anne's Bounty which enabled incumbents to borrow money for repairs, restoration or even building houses for their residency. The amounts available were based on yearly income, no more than three times income could be borrowed, repayable over 30 years at 4%. An application form for Paull exists dated 11th July 1856 and the stated purpose of the £684 loan is for "building". On the form the applicant (probably Rev. George Clifford Pease who was vicar of Paull at the time) names the parish as Paull with Thorngumbald and states the living is a vicarage and not a rectory or perpetual curate. The yearly income is given as:

[88].

	£	s	d
Land Rents	165	7	11
Tithes	88	13	4
Easter Dues	2	8	1
Church Fees	4	4	6
Total	260	13	10

The new vicarage (right), designed by the celebrated architect Cuthbert Brodrick, was built in 1857. By 1928 the vicar of Paull, Dr. J.T. Hutton, was complaining in the public press about the "dilapidations" of the vicarage and the fact that he was expected to pay for its maintenance. By this time Hutton had been the vicar in Paull for seventeen years and had been chaplain to Paull Point Battery during WWI. It was pointed out to the Rev. Hutton that legally as the vicar he was responsible for the maintenance of his vicarage.[89] He threatened to resign, but

remained as vicar of Paull until he retired in 1939. The vicarage was sold in 1946 and the vicar, since the mid 1950s, has lived in Hedon. This former vicarage still stands in Paull and confusingly is called Paull Manor.

Archbishop Herring's 1743 visitation is also useful for providing other details about Paull. It shows there were 35 families in the parish, with only one dissenter, Roger Harrison a papist and no other type of meeting house in the parish. Paull didn't have a public or charity school, but for those who could afford it there were two private schools run by John Buck and Frances Simon who "…both take care to instruct their Scholars in the principles of the Christian Religion & to bring them duly to Church."[90] The only alms/charitable house in the parish was an old house left by Mr. James which the overseers of the poor maintained.

Another visitation, that of Archbishop Drummond in 1764, tells a slightly different story about Paull. By this time the vicar was Joseph Dawson. With 35 families in the parish the population had remained static, but there were now two

dissenters, one a papist (possibly the same family as in 1743) and one a Quaker. There was still no other religious house in the parish apart from the church and now no alms/charitable houses or schools public or private. Dawson, the vicar still lived in Thorngumbald and conducted a service in Paull only once on a Sunday as he also conducted services at Keyingham or Thorngumbald.[91]

The interior of St. Andrew's, Paull still retains some very interesting features such as two beautiful piscinae, one of which has two carved figureheads (left) – one of a man and one of a woman. There is also a colourfully decorated Forster and Andrews organ supplied in June 1903 at a cost of £277,[92] which appears to be still in good condition but leaning slightly. Just inside the door there is a stone carved figure (perhaps an angel) with a shield. The ravages of time have obliterated its details. There is one bell in the church with the inscription "James Harrison, Founder, Barrow, 1788". In addition to this there are several important and interesting monuments inside the church.

Tour of the Church Interior

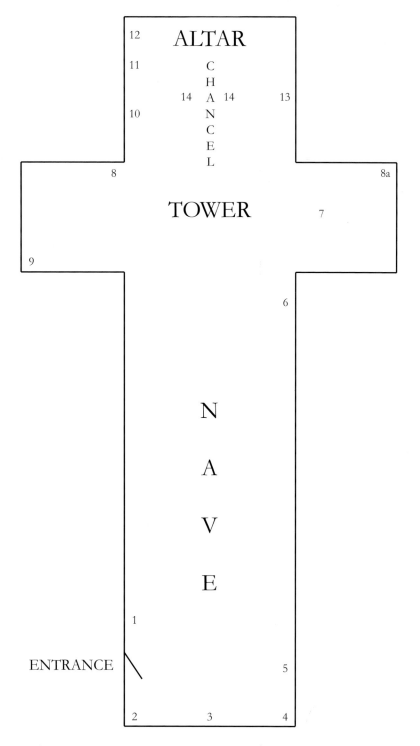

1. Cornelius Stovin Monument
2. Rev. Samuel Jones Window
3. Dorothy Robinson Tomb
4. Barbara Locke Tomb
5. Thomas Locke Charity Plaque
6. James Wray Window
7. Forster & Andrews Organ

8/8a. Two Piscinae with carved figureheads
9. Ombler Monument
10. Blaydes Monument
11. Ann Carvile Monument
12. Stovin Monument
13. Jane Bannister Monument
14. Rev. Cordeaux Inscription

Architecturally the church is of a perpendicular, cruciform shape. It has a nave, chancel, north and south transepts, north and south aisles, pointed octagonal piers in four bay arcades and a tower in three stages with Y tracery. The monuments are listed below, the numbers referring to the accompanying plan (accuracy in recording these monuments has been attempted, but they are sometimes not very legible. Original spelling has been retained, but modern punctuation has sometimes been used to make easier reading):

1) Inside the door (left):

In memory of Cornelius Stovin, late of this Parish. Gentn. Who
died the 19th day of August 1799, aged 31 years and whose
remains are interred underneath this pew.

Below this, slightly to the left is the stone carved figure with the shield.

Inside of door (right):

The Incorporated Society for
Buildings & Churches
Granted £70 AD 1878 Towards
Reseating and Restoring this Church
All the seats are for the Free Use
Of the Parishioners According to
Law

2) Next to this, stained glass window:

To the Glory of God and in Loving Memory of Rev. James Samuel Jones 25 Years Vicar and Curate of this Parish and Sarah His
Wife both of whom rest in the adjacent Church Yard. This Window was Erected 1884.

3) Floor tomb (between pews):

Here Lyeth the Body of Dorothy
The Wife of Mr. Leonard Robinson of
Newton Garth in the County of
York and Daughter of John Lister
Of Linton in the same County Esq.
Who Died The 18th January 1676

4) Diagonally opposite door, railed in tomb:

Sacred to the memory of Barbara wife of Mr. Thos. Locke of Kingston upon Hull. A prudent faithful wife.
A tender affectionate mother. She died 19th Nov 1792 aged 29 years. Leaving two infant sons.

5) Next to this:

Wooden wall plaque

A.D. 1825. Thomas Locke Esquire of Kingston upon Hull bequeathed by his will to the Minister and Churchwarden, for the time being of the Parish of Paghill otherwise Paull in Holderness in the East Riding of the County of York the Sum of Fifty Pounds, four percent annuities upon trust to pay and distribute the dividends and interests thereof half in money and the remainder in bread within the church of Paull aforesaid and as near and as might be to the tomb of his late wife immediately after the Sacrament of Easter Day and Christmas in every year to the most deserving poor persons for the time being residing in the said parish and who do not receive Parochial relief.

6) To the left of this (near organ), stained glass window:

To the Glory of God and in Loving Memory of James Lambert Wray
Of Newton Garth in this Parish who died April 19th 1897 age 32 years
(This window was put in place in April 1903. It was made by Burlison and Gryll of London and depicts the Good Shepherd and the Prodigal Son).

7) The Forster and Andrews organ.

8) The two piscinae, 8a behind the organ has the carved figureheads.

9) In the North Transept:

In memory of John Ombler of Paull
Farmer upwards of 50 years Tenant to B Blaydes Esq. and to his son H Blaydes Esq. of this Parish by whom this Tablet is erected in Regard for a truly honest respectable Man
He died the 8th May 1805 aged 70 years
Sarah his wife died the 1st Aug 1803
Aged 63 years

10) In the Chancel (left side):

Sacred to the memory of Hugh Blaydes Esq. Lord of the Manors of Sutton cum Bransholme and Sculcoates, grandson of James Blaydes and Ann Marvel. His wife Ob. 9th April 1759 ae 74 and of Elizabeth his wife, daughter of Peter de la Pryme of Hatfield in this County Esq. Ob. 21st August 1772 ae 67 leaving three children viz. Hugh Blaydes who died unmarried 8th April 1767 ae 33; Frances Blaydes Ob. 3rd May 1795 ae 65; Benjamin Blaydes of High Paull in this Parish Esq. who died 28th October 1805 ae 71. He married Kitty second daughter and co-heiress of Christopher Scott of Albrough Esq. who died 20th Nov 1782 ae 34 by whom he had four children: Benjamin, Hugh, Catherine, Ann Ob. 24th December 1798 ae 21; and Christopher Ob. 28th May 1783 ae 4. Harriet Elizabeth, the beloved daughter of Hugh Blaydes of High Paull in this Parish and of Ramby Hall in the county of Nottingham Esq. and Delia Maria his wife, daughter of Richard Wood of Hollin Hall in the county of York Esq. departed this life the 9th November 1824 ae 19. Hugh Blaydes Esq. of High Paull in this Parish who died Feby 15th AD 1829 in the 51st year of his age. He was acting magistrate for Nottingham for which county he served the Office of High Sheriff during the alarming disturbances of the Luddites in the year 1812 and was for some time Major in the 3rd West York Militia. Hugh Marvel Blaydes of High Paull who departed this life on the 21st Janry 1836 after a short illness at Halifax Nova Scotia in the 28th year of his age.

11) *Sacred to the Memory of Ann Carvile. Last surviving daughter of Henry and Margaret Carvile of Boreas Hill in this parish. OBt April 18th 1797. Aged 85. "Her virtues walked a narrow round. But seldom paused neer left a void. We trust her Heavenly Master found the single talent well employed."*

12) Open book:

(Left side) *This durable volume is inscribed to the memory of a family whose mortal remains are deposited within the communion rail of the church. "After Life's Fitful Fever They Sleep Well".*

(Right side) *James Stovin Esq. of Boreas Hill M.D. and a Magistrate for the East Riding of the County. OBt. May 22nd 1797 aged 35. Susanna his wife (the only child of Francis and Susanna Carvile) OBt. Novr 18th 1839 aged 76. And their three daughters: Margaret Susanna Maria OBt. Decr 22nd 1808 aged 21. Sara Anne OBt. July 5th 1809 aged 20. And Frances Joanna Elizabeth who died in her infancy.*

13) On the right side of the Chancel:

In memory of Jane third daughter of Anthony Bannister Esquire of High Paull House who departed this life January 7th 1857 aged 15 years.

14) Choir stalls, inscription on front (both sides):

To the Glory of God in memory of St. Andrew and the Rev. R.D.C. Cordeaux Vicar of Paull for 20 years during which the church was restored 1888 R.I.P.

As well as the above existing monuments, the parish registers, which date as far back as 1657, are an interesting source on the history of the area. The original registers can be consulted at the East Riding Archives Office in Beverley, and the East Yorkshire Family History Society has transcribed the gravestones and monuments of Paull Church as part of their Monumental Inscription series of booklets. Therefore, I do not want to merely repeat a list of entries from these sources, however there are one or two entries in the parish records that are of particular interest:

*11th April 1659. Baptism of Laetitia Holme, Daughter of Henry
Holme of Paull Holme and his wife Penelope*

An interesting entry showing that despite the recent troubles of the Civil War, during which the Holme family supported the royalist cause and had their property confiscated, the family had recovered to continue living at Paull Holme.

*20th October 1678 Baptism of Henry, son of Michael Carvile of
Borehouse Hill*

Shows the variant spellings of both the Carvile name (sometimes spelt Carvill or Carvile) and the place of their residence which has been spelt varyingly "Bowerhouse Hill", "Boarhouse Hill" or "Boreas Hill".

2nd May 1819, Lieut James Colquhoun. Aged 68. Formerly of the Third Regiment of Guards and the Royal Invalids in which camps he served in the American War and survived many wounds.

19th March 1840 Burial of the body of a washed up fisherman called William Earl. His name was tattooed on his arm.

7.

Finally, lists of the incumbents of Paull from 1295 to 1947 have survived.[93]

1295, 24th September, Will. de Empringham (Idem) (resigned for the church of Hoton Cranswick) (Idem)

1343, 14th November, Joh. de Kyldale de Brasdale (resigned for the chapel of Nuttal)

1351, 13th October, Joh. de Bildeston (resigned) (Idem)

1359, 15th December, Joh. de Herdeby (Idem)

1399, 20th June, Robt. de Berdesey (resigned for the Vicarage of Aldburgh).

1403, 19th October, Alanus Cotham vel Cochon (died) (Idem)

1427, 10th August, Tho. Chester vd Chese (died) (Idem)

1436, 21st June, Joh. Aunger (resigned) (Idem)

1471, 6th June, Will Baxster (resigned) (Idem)

1475, 16th June, Will Hertford (Idem)

1493, 12th December, Xtpher Billop (died) (Idem)

1504, 12th March, Xtpher Hamerton (died) (Idem)

1517, 11th September, Robt. Pennyng (died) (Idem)

1538, 3rd April, Ric. Perkynson.

Gap

Will Forsett (died)

1598, 6th February, Seth Thomson.

1613, 29th January, Geor. Shawe.

1613, 9th March, Ric. Bradshaw, M.A. (Idem)

1662, 3rd October, Joh. Smithson. (Idem)

1680, 13th October, Henry Holme M.A. (on death of John Smithson).

1690/1, 27th January, William James (collated).

1723, 23rd December, William Robson (on death of William James).

1758, 7th April, John Mackereth (on death of William Robson).

1762, 24th March, John Clarke (on death of last incumbent, not named).

1763, 16th August, Joseph Dawson (on death of John Clarke).

1788, 1st October, John Bennett (on death of Joseph Dawson).

1793, 16th August, Lamplugh Wickham B.A. [assumed surname Hird on 2nd February 1795] (on death of John Bennett).

1843, 3rd February, James Samuel Jones (on death of Lamplugh Hird).

1856, 11th July, George Clifford Pease (on death of James Samuel Jones).

1865, 28th March, Charles Croft Hill M.A. (on cession of G.C. Clifford).

1866, 23rd January, Richard Dymoke Cawdron Cordeaux B.A. (on death of C.C. Hill). Cordeaux died 20th October 1888.

1889, 14th March, Anthony Bathe B.A. (on death of R.D.C. Cordeaux).

1894, 8th November, Charles Henry Piggott (on cession of Anthony Bathe).

1896, 15th February, Horace Rudkin M.A. (on resignation of C.H. Piggott).

1910, 21st June, Marmaduke Alan Prickett M.A. (on death of H. Rudkin).

1911, 15th June, John Thomas Hutton M.A., (on resignation of M.A. Prickett).
Hutton vacated benefice 25th August 1939.

1940, 9th May, James Alfred Couse (vacated benefice 13th April 1946).

1946 Presentation Suspended.

1947, 24th November, Curate in Charge Charles Edward Dunn B.A., united with Hedon.

The Torre manuscript also contains the following information about the church:

"The Church and Tythes of S. Mary and S. Andrew of Pagula or Paul-Holme were given by Stephen, Earl of Albermarle, to the Abbay of Albermarle in Normandy, viz., to the Cell of Birstall belonging to the same, and on 10th Oct., 18th Ric. II was granted by the Abbat and Convent of St. Martyn of Albermarle to the Abbay of Kirkstall, after the dissolution of which, on 31 Oct. 5th and 6th Philip and Mary, it was granted to Nicholas, Archbishop of York, and his successors." Torre also listed some "testamentary burials" among which were the following:

1501. 16th August. Wm. Holme, gent, to be buried in the Churchyard of Holme.

1503. 9th November. Robert Holme, of Paul Holme, Esq., to be buried in the Quere, before the image of Our Blessed Lady.

1510. 23rd May. Mary Holme, of Pauleholme, to be buried in the Quere.

1565. 23rd June. John Holme, of Paule Holme, Esq., to be buried in the church among his ancestors.

1631. 8th February. Henry Holme, of Paule Holme, Esq., to be buried in the church.

It is interesting that Torre places the church at Paull Holme as well as mentioning a churchyard at Holme and then a church implying that these latter two were different locations. However, Torre was writing in the late 17th century long after the events he is describing and with ancient documents that may not have been clear. In addition to this it is possible that vicar serving the parish church of Paull also served the private church/chapel of the Holme family.

James Torre was born in April 1649 and baptised at Haxey in Lincolnshire. He attended school at Belton and was admitted to Magdalene College, Cambridge in 1666. For reasons unknown he moved to York and carried out extensive research on the ecclesiastical history of Yorkshire and it is amongst this research (completed in five volumes) that the above list of Paull incumbents is found. Torre married twice, but only his second marriage in 1694 to Anna Lister from Leeds, produced a child (named Nicholas) in 1695. In 1699 Torre purchased the manor of Syndale near Wakefield, but he was not resident there for long as he died on 31st July that year. It is a coincidence that a descendant of James Torre (also called James) married Betty Holme, daughter of Stephen Holme of Paull Holme; this Torre branch of the family inherited Paull Holme in 1811 (see Chapter 2 for further details).

Non-conformist Chapels

Dissent from the English church has been extant in Paull from at least the 18th century. The *Victoria County History* covering Paull also mentions Catholicism being practised in the village from the 16th century, Quakers meeting there from around 1670 and refers to houses being registered for dissent in 1812.[94] The Toleration Act of 1689 allowed dissenting groups to hold public meetings so long as they were registered with the diocese or with the courts. The meetings could either be in a whole building or just a room of a building (for example someone's house). Some records for these registrations have survived from the late 18th century and these show that in March 1797 the house of William Stokesley in Paull was registered for meetings.[95] Unfortunately the records do not tell us what denomination the dissenting houses are, but it is interesting that dissent came so early to a small village such as Paull.

Paull has two non-conformist buildings standing today, both chapels connected to Methodism. The first, a Wesleyan chapel (overleaf), opened in 1805 and after being "…closed for many years…"[96] was restored in 1912 and: "The recently re-opened chapel continues to be well attended…".[97] According to the 1851 Religious Census for Yorkshire the chapel had 80 free sittings and 40 other sittings and was a separate and entire building used exclusively for worship. Its average congregation was 60, but on 30th March 1851 there were 96 people in attendance at the service. This Wesleyan chapel still stands but is no longer used for services.

The other chapel was a Primitive Methodist chapel. Primitive Methodism was a breakaway group from the Wesleyan movement, which began in 1811 and was particularly popular with agricultural labourers, miners and the poor of the

towns and cities. It spread quickly and the first chapel in the East Riding (if we exclude Hull) was at North Cave in 1819.[98] Paull's first Primitive Methodist chapel was opened in 1851, but it was only a small building and so could only hold a small congregation. According to the 1851 Religious Census for Yorkshire Paull's Primitive Methodist Chapel was a separate building used purely as a place of worship; average attendance at services over the previous year had been 35, but on Sunday 30th March 1851 there were 57 in the congregation. Due to its limited space the chapel did not last long and was demolished in 1871. A new Primitive Methodist chapel was opened in the same year on a different site with the stone for it laid on 21st August 1871. The meeting for the stone laying was held at the Paull Wesleyan chapel demonstrating there was some co-operation between the two dissenting movements. A large crowd attended the ceremony travelling by "…a large bus…a keel…a passenger steamer, besides the train to Hedon."[99] By this time £76 had been raised for the chapel building fund and at the ceremony bricks were also laid. Presiding over the event was George Dunhill Moxon of High Paull House. After the ceremony tea was laid on at his residence where "The large rooms of the house were filled, and tables were set out in the garden".[100] In August 1912 the chapelgoers held a social event to raise funds to paint and renovate the chapel. At it "A novel feature was the tea, at which the famous Paull shrimps were the principle edibles."[101] The total raised was £10 10s.

Some of the Primitive Methodist Connexion Circuit records have survived and the 1871 schedule shows that Paull Chapel was built in 1871, was freehold property and there were 74 lettable and 76 free seats. About 130 people attended services out of a population of 400 in the area. It cost £241, 14s, 2d to build of which £125 still had to be paid; the pew rents were earning £8, 11s, 3d per annum and there were fifteen trustees of the chapel. By 1875 the outstanding debt was £65, but there were now only twelve trustees and attendances at services had gone down to 110 which meant the pew rents were now only earning £7, 10s, 10d per annum, despite the population of the area having had increased to 496. The nearby Hedon Primitive Chapel was faring much worse, with seating for 162, but attendances only about 80. Perhaps the lower attendances at Paull were also affecting the finances of the chapel as the balance sheet for the 1875 schedule shows that the income was £26, 15s, 4d but the expenditure was £29, 4s, 6d.[102] This decline possibly continued as the chapel closed in 1915. By 1926 local shop owner Benjamin Race had bought the chapel and was converting it into two cottages,[103] which still stand today.

References – Chapter 5

68 *The Hull Times*, 25th February 1928, p. 14.

69 Ibid.

70 Calendar of Patent Rolls Preserved in the Public Record Office, Edward III, vol. X, A.D. 1354-1358. London, 1909, p. 271.

71 Poulson, George. *The History and Antiquities of the Seigniory of Holderness in the East Riding of the County of York*. Hull, 1841.

72 Tickell, George. *History of the Town and County of Kingston Upon Hull*. 1796, p. 484.

73 Glynne, Sir Stephen, Bart. "Notes on Yorkshire Churches", *Yorkshire Archaeological Journal*. Vol. 26, 1921-22, p. 281.

74 Bulmer, T. *History, Topography and Directory of East Yorkshire (with Hull)*. Ashton on Ribble, 1892.

75 *Hull Times*, 23rd August, 1913, p. 8.

76 Pevsner, Nikolaus and Neave, David. *The Buildings of England Yorkshire: York and the East Riding*. 2nd ed. London, 1995, p. 645.

77 Hull Bench Books, Hull City Archives at the Hull History Centre, BRB4.

78 *Hull Times*, 5th May, 1877, p. 3.

79 *Hull Times*, 19th May, 1877, p. 3.

80 Glynne, Sir Stephen, Bart. "Notes on Yorkshire Churches", *Yorkshire Archaeological Journal*. Vol. 26, 1921-22, p. 281.

81 *Hull Times*, 16th August, 1879, p. 6.

82 *Hull Times*, 14th April 1928, p. 12.

83 *Hull Advertiser*, 24th February, 1832, p. 3.

84 *Hull Advertiser*, 4th January, 1839.

85 Ibid.

86 Kent, G.H.R. "Paull", Allison, K.J. (ed.) *The Victoria History of the Counties of England: a History of the County of York, East Riding, vol. v, Holderness: Southern Part*. Oxford, 1984, p. 125.

87 *Yorkshire Archaeological Society Record Series*, vol. 75, p. 10.

88 Taken from document MD109 held by the Borthwick Institute of Historical Research, University of York.

89 *The Hull Times*, 31st March 1928, p. 5.

90 *Yorkshire Archaeological Society Record Series*, vol. 75, p. 10.

91 Annesley, Cressida and Hoskin, Philippa. *Archbishop Drummond's Visitation Returns 1764 II: Yorkshire H-R*. York, 1998, p. 170.

92 Forster and Andrews Business Archive. Ledger 09, entry 1308, page 128 (in the Hull Local Studies Library at the Hull History Centre).

93 The entries for 1295 to 1662 are taken from the *Torre Manuscript* held by the York Minster Archives. The entries 1680 – to 1947 are taken from Document Add MS 169 held by the Borthwick Institute of Historical Research, University of York.

94 Kent, G.H.R. "Paull", Allison, K.J. (ed.) *The Victoria History of the Counties of England: a History of the County of York, East Riding, vol. v, Holderness: Southern Part*. Oxford, 1984, p. 126.

95 Borthwick Institute of Historical Research, University of York. "Summary List of Certificates of Dissenters' Meeting Houses". May 1986, p. 54.

96 *Hull Times*, 23rd August 1913, p. 8.

97 *Hull Times*, 14th September 1912, p. 9.

98 Neave, David and Susan. *East Riding Chapels and Meeting House*. East Yorkshire Local History Society, 1990, p. 13.

99 *Eastern Morning News*, 22nd August 1871, p. 4.

100 Ibid.

101 *Hull Times*, 24th August, 1912, p. 9.

102 A large volume collection now in the keeping of the Hull Local Studies Library at the Hull History Centre.

103 *The Hull Times*, 11th September 1926, p. 7.

CHAPTER 6: PUBLIC HOUSES

The Humber Tavern is the oldest pub in Paull and was built in 1805. In 1808 the keeper of the tavern attempted to attract visitors from Hull with a bathing machine:

BATHING .[104]

Robert Wright, of the Humber Tavern…Paull…respectfully…informs his Friends and the Public in general, that he has provided a BATHING MACHINE, so constructed as to combine every convenience with perfect safety and privacy. Paul is pleasantly situated on the Humber, a short distance from Hull; and a packet boat sails regularly between these places, three or four times a week. A gun ship and frigate are building within ten minutes walk of the Humber Tavern. R. Wright embraces this opportunity to return his most sincere Thanks to the public, for the favours they have already been pleased to honour him with, and is determined that no exertion shall be wanting to merit a continuance of the same.

In 1814 the Humber Tavern was up for sale and the advert provides details about the size and layout of the pub. On the ground floor there were two large parlours, two kitchens, a bar and a cellar; the first floor had a large sitting room, three bedrooms as well as ceiled garrets.[105]

At the end of May 1835 a fire broke out in the upper part of the pub and "…a message was immediately dispatched to Hull for assistance. The Yorkshireman and Wincolmlee fire engines were quickly sent off, but were met on the road by a messenger who informed them that the fire was extinuished without causing any serious damage." [106]

By 1836 Trinity House were renting a room in the Humber Tavern for the showing of a light as an aid to shipping prior to building the Paull Lighthouse.

The Royal Oak (overleaf, above right) is the second oldest pub in the village. Its exact date is unknown, but it was certainly in existence by 1823.[107] A tragedy happened at the public house in September 1881 when Elizabeth Milsom, the 29 year old wife of the publican, hung herself in her bedroom in the pub and her body was discovered by her own mother. The inquest heard evidence that she had been depressed for some time and the jury delivered a verdict of "Suicide whilst in a state of temporary insanity".

In February 1953 storms caused severe flooding along the coast. The landlord at the time, Montague Bunting, had to jam the back door with cases of beer to hold back the water. Drinkers in the bar wore sea boots and helped to brush water back outside. The following day Mr. Bunting had to retrieve coal from the mud flats in order to light fires as his own two tons had been swept away by the floods.

The Crown Inn (below) is Paull's third public house and was opened around 1865 opposite the Humber Tavern by James Stark who was at the petty sessions in September 1864 applying for a liquor licence for the pub. The Crown may have been converted from part of a row of Georgian cottages.[108]

The landladies of these two latter pubs found themselves in trouble in June 1903 as:

"Mrs. Hass and Mrs. Pickering, the respective landladies of the Royal Oak and Crown Inn, Paull, appeared before the magistrates at the Hedon petty sessions…to receive judgement in a recent prosecution…In the case of Mrs. Pickering, the analysis of the spirit showed a deficiency of 10 per cent, and she was fined 20s. The deficiency was not so great in the case of Mrs. Hass, being 2.6 per cent, and a fine of 10s was imposed".[109]

There are newspaper references to other public houses in Paull. *The Hull Packet* for 12th June 1810 advertises the auction of the "…Inn, known by the sign of the Grapes…" currently owned by Robert Wright. This pub had two sitting rooms, tap room, bar, kitchen, dining room and "suitable lodgings" which were "…lofty and pleasant, most of them commanding Humber views". Much is made of the "…recent establishment of a yard at Paul, for building men of war…" increasing the value of the property. The pub also had a stable yard, wharf and bathing machines. However, there is no clear indication of where exactly the pub was situated in Paull other than it backed on to the Humber as it had a wharf.

The *Hull Advertiser* mentions another public house whose location isn't known:

John Watson .[110]

Late of the Ship Inn, Paull, near Hedon

Begs leave most respectfully to inform his friends and the Public in general, that he has Removed to a more commodious House at the end of the Village next the Ship Yard, where it will be his constant study to merit (by the most diligent attention to his Customers) a continuance of that Patronage of which he has already received so liberal a share.

Perhaps it was one of the other public houses in the village and was renamed. It also isn't clear which public house Watson has moved to. The phrases "more commodious" and "end of the village" would indicate the Humber Tavern as this would fit both descriptions. However, "next the ship yard" is a generous term for the Humber Tavern's location as it is still some distance from the ship yard site. Perhaps Watson was indicating that there were no other buildings between his new public house and the shipyard.

References – Chapter 6

[104] *Hull Advertiser*, 23rd July 1808.

[105] *Hull Advertiser*, 13th August 1814.

[106] *Hull Advertiser*, 2nd June 1835.

[107] Baines, Edward. *Baines's Yorkshire: History, Directory and Gazatteer of the County of York Vol. 2 East and North Ridings*. East Ardsley, 1969, p. 376.

[108] *The Victoria History of the Counties of England: a History of Yorkshire East Riding Vol. V, Holderness: Southern Part*. Oxford University Press, 1984, p. 114.

[109] *East Yorkshire Telegraph*, 13th June 1903.

[110] *Hull Advertiser*, 22nd July 1809, p. 2.

CHAPTER 7: CORK MODELS AND SKELETONS

BATTERSBY'S MUSEUM AT PAULL

Battersby Museum

Bulmer and Miles and Richardson[111] mention a museum in Paull run by a Mr. James David Battersby who is described as an ex-Hull town councillor. Battersby's life can be traced through parish registers, census returns, directories, electoral registers, council minutes and newspapers from his birth to his death and he seems to have had a varied life. He was born on the 28th January 1836; his parents George and Elizabeth lived on Sisson's Row, Hull and his father was a smith. George Battersby and Elizabeth Dunn had married on the 1st January 1834 in Sculcoates Parish and the young James was christened on 28th February 1836, also in Sculcoates Parish.[112] The 1841 census finds the family living on Scott Street, an area the Battersby family would stay in for a long time. According to the 1851 census fifteen year old James was living at 2 Ebenezer Place with his widowed father and a housekeeper, showing that young James had lost his mother. By now he was an apprentice gilder. Battersby next appears in White's Hull Directory for 1858 when he was a gilder on Scott Street. According to the 1861 census James, now 25, was the head of the household at 1 Ebenezer Terrace, married to Maria (also aged 25), with a 3 year old daughter. His occupation is given as "painter, gilder" and his widowed father lives with them. By 1867 *White's Hull Directory* describes him as a clothes and furniture broker on Wincolmlee. The 1871 census finds him living at 41 Wincolmlee with his wife and still only the one child; his father is still living with him and Battersby's occupation is given as "general broker". The Hull electoral registers for this period describe his business premises as being on Lincoln Street. *Kelly's 1872 North and East Ridings of Yorkshire Directory* still lists him as a general broker on Lincoln Street as does *Kelly's 1879 North and East Ridings Directory*, but his home address by this time is given as Stanley Villa, Hornsea. Disaster struck at Battersby's Lincoln Street premises in 1868 when a fire broke out late at night and "The stock was entirely destroyed, and the building gutted…".[113] The total loss was £400, but Battersby was only insured for £150.

Battersby was back in Hull by 1881 at Rose Cottage (the first house past Sculcoates Lane on Beverley Road) and the census describes him as auctioneer and valuer. He is living there with his wife Maria and a servant called Margaret Clark. In 1882, according to *Kelly's Hull Directory*, Battersby is now an auctioneer, valuer, surveyor and estate and commission agent at 7 Scale Lane, but still resident at Rose Cottage. In *Atkinson's 1888 Hull and District Directory* he is a ship chandler on High Street. Despite earlier unsuccessful attempts in 1874 and 1876, Battersby's civic service as a Hull councillor seems to have been a fairly short period around 1880. In 1879 he is a councillor for the East

Sculcoates ward and he continues to appear at council meetings in 1880 and 1881. However, by 1882 he is no longer a councillor and he does not appear again on the Hull council.

Battersby is not listed in Paull until the *1889 Kelly's North and East Ridings of Yorkshire Directory* which is the first entry for his museum in the village. At this time it cost 3d to enter it. Now aged 54 in the 1891 census he is listed as living at Pier House, Paull and described as a "Ship breaker's agent" with his wife and Ada Campling who is 19 years old and whose relationship in the household is described as daughter. Also in the house is 9 year old James Wood who is described as grandson. It is possible that Battersby has remarried; the 1891 census isn't very clear and his wife's name appears to be Annie. Previously Battersby and his wife have been the same age; now he is 54 and she is 40. Battersby had certainly remarried by the time of the 1901 census; still living at Pier House Paull, he now lived with his 50 year old wife Rachel Ann (this age fits that of the wife given on the 1891 census as does the name Ann), his 19 year old grandson

James Wood, a 6 year old granddaughter called Dorothy Campling and a 16 year old niece called Gertrude Naylor. His occupation is given as shipowner and ship breaker. In the directory entries for Paull, Battersby is often listed as a shipbreaker and antique dealer with references to him living at Pier House; Bulmer also has him listed as a machinery breaker. A newspaper feature on Paull in 1913 describes Battersby's shipbreaking business acumen: "His first business venture of any magnitude was when he bought the Emerald Isle, a big passenger and cargo boat, plying between Hull and the Continent. Many there were who ridiculed his venture and prophesied financial failure. But Mr. Battersby amply vindicated his business acumen…for although the first cost of the boat was £1,050, and although it took 40 men and boys nine months to knock the ship to pieces, it proved a remunerative speculation."[114]

In addition to this he was serving as a parish councillor for Paull. The museum seems to have closed by 1914. In January 1912 the following piece appeared in the *Hull Times*: "The popular Councillor J.D. Battersby, Pier House, received many congratulations, including one from Malta, on attaining his 78th birthday on Monday."[115] This doesn't quite fit the ages given on the censuses or his birth date. James David Battersby died in August 1914, the obituary appeared in the *Hull Times* on 15th August. The funeral was on Sunday 9th August at Paull Church with the service conducted by the local vicar J.T. Hutton. Directories until 1919 list a Mrs. Battersby at Paull, but make no mention of the museum suggesting that it closed down around the time of his death and the building itself, at some point, was demolished. It had certainly gone by 1922.[116] It had stood near the current Hepworth's shipyard in Paull.

Describing the museum and its proprietor one reporter observed: "Men of kindred tastes may find there much that is valuable and entertaining; but, unfortunately, moth and dust have wrought sad havoc with the natural history specimens, and the exhibition, which is on view for a small charge, is not so interesting to the general public as it might be made. But Mr. Battersby is a collector first, and a showman afterwards."[117] Among the collections of the museum were a facsimile of the death warrant of Charles I; an original brick from the walls of Hull; a model of the first smack built in Hull; the tiller of the ferry boat that ran between Grimsby and Paull; the speaking trumpet of the Zephyr (the first yacht of Trinity House); a cork model of the Hull Town Hall made by an old customs officer; the old signboard of the Garibaldi Inn, Beverley; a collection of Wedgwood; and a stuffed horse skin said to be an officer's horse involved in the Indian mutiny. The most interesting exhibit was the complete skeleton of Miss Jenkins,

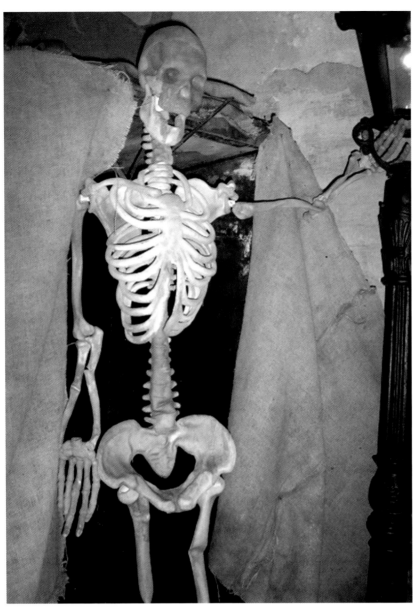

aka "Rabbit Nanny" (left). She was a hawker of rabbits on the streets of Hull and it is claimed that her piercing call could be heard as far away as Barton upon Humber and 4 miles distant. She had sold her body to medical science for the price of £5. The skeleton was purchased at the sale of effects of Dr. Hay. Our reporter observed of this skeleton: "The most remarkable feature about this skeleton is the unusually large capacity of the chest, from which the extraordinary bust measurement of this old Hull resident may be easily imagined. This unusual development explains the great lung power for which she was celebrated."[118]

On the closure of Battersby's museum Rabbit Nanny's skeleton found a new home at Paull Point Battery where it was used to play pranks on unsuspecting passers-by when they dressed it in a sheet with only the skull exposed; it was a talking point in Paull for many years. The skeleton still hangs there today at the recently created Fort Paull Museum.

These exhibits do not really sound like antiques or much of a museum. They sound more like the junk Battersby would collect as a shipbreaker and we can not be surprised that Mrs. Battersby was glad to get rid of them after her husband's death.

References – Chapter 7

[111] Bulmer, T. *History, Topography and Directory of East Yorkshire (with Hull).* Ashton on Ribble, 1892, p477. and: Miles, George T. and Richardson, William. *A History of Withernsea with Notices of Other Parishes in South Holderness in the East Riding of the County of York.* Hull, 1911, p. 215.

[112] International Genealogical Index online at www.familysearch.org

[113] *Hull Packet*, 3rd July 1868

[114] *Hull Times*, 23rd August 1913, p. 8.

[115] *Hull Times*, 3rd February 1912, p. 9.

[116] *Hull Times*, 5th August 1922, p. 5.

[117] *Hull Times*, 5th October 1904, p. 2.

[118] Ibid.

CHAPTER 8: TRADE AND OCCUPATIONS

Trade and occupation in Paull has relied mainly on agriculture since the medieval period (as it does today) although between 1825 and 1855 there was a brickyard in the village. However, there are references as early as 1200 to Paull being a port when the Count of Aumale was dealing in port related activities; ferries also ran from Paull to Lincolnshire. Fishing also seems to have been undertaken from the medieval period, in 1377[119] there were twelve seamen in Paull. The 1851 census lists 27 fishermen in Paull and in 1912 there were nineteen men working thirteen boats, but by 1923 this had declined to six small boats.[120] In the 19th and 20th centuries Paull was particularly renowned for its shrimp fishing: "Any child in Hull will tell you that Paull is celebrated for its shrimps, and any boating man is likely to take an interest in the place on account of the smartly handled little craft by which the aforementioned shrimps are caught. These cutter-rigged craft, varying from about six to twelve tons displacement – all worked single-handed – and a few of about fifteen to twenty tons which carry double crew."[121]

A typical Paull shrimper was a rig and hull type with the cockpit well continuing beyond the after part of the mast; very little deck gear was carried; the sails were made by the fishermen themselves with a lot of flow and they were made to last a long time. The shrimpers tended to stay close to home, occasionally sailing out to the Haile Sands or even up the Trent and Ouse.

During the Napoleonic Wars Thomas Steemson was building warships at Paull in a yard on the bank of the Humber close to Paull Point Battery. The *Proserpine*, a 909 ton frigate with 42 guns, built by the yard was launched in August 1807. Bad weather prevented the launch taking place and many went away disappointed, but some stayed in Paull overnight and 300 to 400 people eventually watched the launch take place between 6 am and 7 am. One boy on his return home on crossing Hedon Haven fell in to it. The haven was at its full tide and the water high and "Several perfons were prefent, but unable to give him any affiftance and he mufft inevitably have been drowned in a few minutes…"[122] (Sic.) Lieutenant Walker of the 15th Regiment was on recruiting duty in the area and jumped in to the haven rescuing the boy.

In January 1812 the *Apollo*, built for the East India Company, was launched at Paull. Also built in 1812 was the *Anson*, a 74 gun warship costing £140,000, its full length 206 feet 3 inches, the keel length 164 feet, the gun deck 176 feet long and its breadth 47 feet 6 inches. A report in *Hull Rockingham* described how between 2,000 and 5,000 persons assembled for the launch of the *Anson*.[123]

Directories of the period suggest that when Benjamin Blaydes, the younger, bought High Paull House in 1769 he had a shipyard there. However, there is no evidence of this. Hugh Blaydes (Benjamin's son) sold part of the estate in 1818 and a shipyard is mentioned in this sale, but this would have been Steemson's yard. A written history of the Blaydes family contains many details of their shipyards and shipbuilding activities, but it has no information about such activities at Paull.[124]

Shipbuilding in Paull went in to decline around 1821 and this had a severe effect on the village. However, a shipyard in Paull was opened as recently as 1940 and still operates.

Paull may have been close to Hull, but there has never been a rail link and no direct road to the village from Hull until the 1930s. Visitors had to make their way via the roads to Hedon and Thorngumbald or tramp across the marshy land of Marfleet and Saltend on foot. Consequently the village had to be self-supporting with its own carriers, grocers, blacksmiths, shoemakers, joiners, butchers and public houses. The Hulme family seem to have carried out different functions in the village. In the far left of the picture below there is a man and child on the doorstep of a building with a bicycle wheel on the wall.

William Hulme, is listed as being a shopkeeper in Paull from 1904 until 1908. From then on he is listed as a cycle repairer. William Hulme and Son are listed as engineers from 1915 until 1926, when they disappear from the village. Dudley Hulme, blacksmith and possibly a relation, is listed from 1910 until 1929 when he too disappears from the village.

References – Chapter 8

[119] *The Victoria History of the Counties of England: a History of Yorkshire East Riding Vol. V, Holderness: Southern Part.* Oxford University Press, 1984, p. 123.

[120] Ibid.

[121] *Humber Yawl Club Year Book*, 1904.

[122] *Hull Advertiser*, 8th August 1807, p. 4.

[123] *Hull Rockingham*, 16th May, 1812.

[124] Bibby, Frances. *The Blaydes – Shipbuilders of Hull.* 1996.

Predating the 1834 Poor Law Amendment Act which created poor law unions, Paull had its own workhouse which was in existence in the 1820s and 1830s. A Poor Law Act had existed since the reign of Elizabeth I, but it was the General Workhouse Act of 1723 and Gilbert's Act of 1782 that allowed parishes to unite and build workhouses and it was under this latter act that Paull acquired its workhouse. The agreement to build the workhouse had been given in the July Quarter Sessions of 1819. The cost of maintaining the poor had been steadily rising in the early nineteenth century and by 1819 Paull was spending £504 8s 9d on its poor, but with the creation of the workhouse this had dramatically reduced by 1834 to £308 19s 3d. This reduction in spending on the poor came at the right time as there was a severe depression in the shipbuilding industry between 1821 and 1831 which would have affected the village. The workhouse at Paull united the parishes of Paull, Keyingham, Thorngumbald and Ryhill. In November 1820 this newspaper advert appeared:

[126]

> Wanted immediately, a steady, intelligent, industrious woman to take the management of a house containing the poor of four united parishes. Also a middle aged man to superintend the woollen manufactory and to assist in the house occasionally. Testimonials as to the character of the person applying for honesty, sobriety, and regularity of conduct, will be required.
>
> Apply to Mr. Wm. Liddle, Paull.

Liddle, an overseer of the poor in Paull, had strong views on how the poor should be managed believing that: "The best mode of managing the able-bodied Labourers is by reducing their families by taking their children into the Workhouse until their wages will maintain them." He also stated that pauper children should be placed with the ratepayers of the Parish as "…this would improve their habits and morals, as they would then be brought up with industry."

According to Smith there were 33 inmates in the course of 1821.[127] According to Mitchelson it cost 2s 6d per week to keep the boarders in the workhouse; in 1826 £215 3s 8d was spent on food at Paull, most of it on meat, flour, potatoes and skimmed milk with smaller amounts spent on tea, butter and oatmeal.[128]

Some of the records of Paull Workhouse have survived (held in University of Hull Archives). They do not show such high figures of inmates for other years and in fact there were never many boarders, as they were called, in the workhouse at any one time. Between the 30th June and 28th July 1827 there were no boarders at all. Between 28th July and 25th August 1827 there was only one, Mary Kirby, staying for twelve days (although she was back in October 1827 staying for 28 days). A typical number for any one period seems to be about six and this implies that the workhouse was only small, it was probably just a converted cottage. I haven't searched all the records but the longest stay I have found was that of John Martin and his wife for 50 days between June and July 1826. The total cash received for boarders in the year ending 31st March 1828 was just £15 8s; the following year it was over £24; in 1831 and 1832 the figure seemed to be stable at just over £46, reducing in 1833 to £34. The parish registers for Paull show that there were 21 illegitimate children born in the village probably because the overseers of the poor made unmarried pregnant women enter the workhouse (though they didn't stay in there for very long), but they may not all have been from Paull itself. The overseers were keen to find the fathers and enforce Bastardy Orders on them in an attempt to make them pay for the upkeep of their offspring. One such example is that of William Garnett of Winestead who failed to appear at the October Quarter Sessions in 1838; in his absence he was declared the father of Sarah Stephenson's child and ordered to pay 1s 6d per week until the child was seven years old. The workhouse records do not survive for this period, but Sarah Stephenson had given birth to two other illegitimate children in it in 1832 and 1834. These amounts were not enough to cover the full cost of raising children and the parish overseers were often paying up to an extra shilling a week to support illegitimate children. Unfortunately the one piece of information the records don't give is any indication of is where the workhouse was. The only clue is from W.R. Watkinson who states: "In several of the larger villages…workhouses were in existence long before the Union was formed (that at Paull is now a public house with cottages attached)."[129] The Humber Tavern and Royal Oak were already public houses when the workhouse was operational at Paull so maybe Watkinson was referring to the Crown Inn, the last of Paull's pubs and not opened until the 1860s which might have been converted from the workhouse. However, there is evidence that the Royal Oak has been extended and taken over a cottage next to it, so this also could be the location of the workhouse.

The Paull Workhouse closed on the 14th November 1838 when the boarders were moved to the new workhouse at Patrington which had been created under the Poor Law Amendment Act of 1834. By 1840 the Patrington Poor Law Union Board were providing indoor relief for one male, two females and eight children and outdoor relief for six males, twelve females and eight children all from Paull. The larger number of females and children may indicate that illegitimacy was still a problem in the village. The cost of this relief was £13 10s for the indoor relief and £30 5s 6d for the outdoor relief. Under this new Poor Law system, the costs of providing for the poor of Paull were still cheaper than the parish providing its own workhouse.

The white cottage in this picture was originally next to the Royal Oak public house and has provided an extension to the pub. It is possible that this cottage was formerly the Paull Workhouse.

References – Chapter 9

[125] I am indebted to the following work for much of the information obtained here, particularly the facts and figures of the workhouse: Oliver, Margaret S. *Poverty and People: an investigation into recipients of poor relief in Holderness, with special reference to the united parishes of Paull, Thorngumbald, Ryhill and Keyingham.* May, 2003. (Dissertation submitted for B.A. Hons in Historical Studies, University of Hull)

[126] *Hull Advertiser*, November 1820.

[127] Smith, M.H. *Poverty in Holderness 1700-1850.* 1968, p. 59.

[128] Mitchelson, N. *The Old Poor Law in East Yorkshire.* East Yorkshire Local History Society. 1953, p. 14.

[129] Watkinson, W.H. *The Relieving Officer Looks Back: the Last Years of Poor Law in Holderness.* 1955, p. 8.

CHAPTER 10: PAULL AIRFIELD

Yes there really was an airfield at Paull situated along Newlands, the road to Oxgoddes Farm and Little Humber and even today it can be clearly defined in the landscape of the area (above). Paull Airfield opened in October 1967 and was the creation of the East Yorkshire Aero Company Ltd. This company had been formed in 1959 with Neville Medforth, a Hull businessman, as its managing director. The company's original intention had been to operate from the old Hedon Aerodrome which it was already leasing, but they had been refused permission on the grounds that it would be a danger to nearby industrial sites with a "Saltend firm" being the chief objector.[130] On 10th February 1960 a public inquiry was held at the Guildhall in Hull following an appeal by the East Yorkshire Aero Company against the decision. At the inquiry it was stated that Hull Corporation had obtained the Hedon Aerodrome site with the intention of creating a city airport, but the war had interrupted these plans. However, Hull Corporation had not abandoned the idea of flying taking place from the aerodrome and there was debate as to whether this intended use could be considered lapsed or not. On the final day of the enquiry John Howlett, managing director of the Distillers Company Ltd., voiced his concerns about the potential dangers of airplanes crashing into the company site at Saltend saying this could cause "...a devastating outbreak of fire and explosion."[131] The public enquiry decision came in October 1960, but did not find in favour of the East Yorkshire Aero Company with the main reason cited being the danger to nearby industry at Saltend.

Having failed at Hedon, the East Yorkshire Aero Company needed to find an alternative location and so, after also trying Hutton Cranswick and Wyton Bar, the site at Oxgoddes Farm was chosen. The company was given permission by East Riding County Council to operate an airfield for the purposes of a flying club and chartered air services. Five fields were amalgamated to create a 1,000 ft grass runway. The three original directors of the company were Neville Medforth, Battle of Britain pilot Squadron Leader "Ginger" Lacey and Michael Heathcote. From the start they hoped that the airfield would be used by the businessmen of Hull and the surrounding area and that small planes with ten to fifteen passengers would be able to use the field. They also intended that the airfield would be used for flying lessons and as the base of a flying club. However, the commercial side of the venture would have to wait a few months as a Board of Trade flying licence for the site would have to be obtained. Privately owned planes and the Hull Aero Club could use the site immediately.

The Hull Aero Club was not a new one, it had existed before WWII, but at the outbreak of war it had disbanded and it had taken until now (despite previous attempts) for it to reform and find a new home. The club reformed following a newspaper appeal by its secretary Ken Charles. Many of the club's members were ex-RAF pilots like founder member John Wardale of Wyton Bar who had flown with Bomber Command between 1938-45. Another member of the club, Neville Medford (also a director of the East Yorkshire Aero Company), bought the hut for the clubhouse and supplied a lot of war surplus material to help get them started. The airfield itself had been created by "…a squad of willing workers, including farmers, tyre fitters, grocers, electrical engineers and others who are prepared to come along every weekend, take off their shirts and get down to work."[132]

However, plans for air transport use at Paull had been mooted as early as 1929, and the *Eastern Morning News* for the 13th June carried an article which spoke of Hull Corporation's plan to rent a site on land owned by the War Office for a seaplane base. This site was said to be close to the bank of the Humber, so was probably situated at High Paull where there were government military installations. The idea was that passengers from Europe would arrive at Paull on a seaplane and then transfer to the Hedon Aerodrome, just two and a half miles away, to catch a standard plane and continue their journey across the Atlantic. However, these plans were never carried out.

At the beginning of January 1969 Bristow Helicopters were operating from the Oxgoddes site, flying supplies to North Sea oil rigs, having moved from Tetney in Lincolnshire after their base there had closed. By this time the airfield had obtained its flying licence under the operating name of Paull Aerodrome, Hull. The Hull Aero Club, with its 130 members, had built a clubhouse and hangar on the site and were now waiting for the arrival of one Condor and two Auster airplanes. By June they were able to employ a full-time flying instructor and offer flying lessons to the public. A course of lessons cost £250, but could be paid for on the "never, never". Would-be pilots had to have a medical first and then were given lessons on a Rollason Condor plane (call sign: Romeo Charlie). The first nine hours were on dual instruction followed by a 20 minute solo flight before returning to dual instruction. After approximately 45 hours of instruction the trainee pilot could take a test to obtain a pilot's licence. The Bridlington Aero Club also used the Paull Airfield as their base. Charter flights were still not running from the site due to the lack of runway flares, but Humber Airways Ltd. owned by the Ellerman Wilson Line planned to be in operation there later that year.

However, the new airfield was already encountering trouble. The residents of Thorngumbald petitioned local councilors with 300 letters in the autumn of 1969 over plans to give the airfield a new ten year lease, their objections based on noise pollution and the effect on property prices. However, following an investigative visit by East Riding councilors the airfield was given permission to operate until at least 1976. Further problems arose in June 1970 when Neville Medforth said he could no longer provide financial support for the site without a return on his money; he was frustrated at the lack of support from residents, the council and air service companies. This marked the end of his thirteen year attempt to create an airfield on the north bank of the Humber. His withdrawal left the Hull Aero Club having to find £1,000 a year to run the site.

By August 1970 there was new hope for the airfield. Humber Airways, based at the Hawker Siddeley site in Brough, would need to find a new base once the Capper Pass chimney was built as its height would prevent them from flying at Brough, but changes to the runway and radio navigation installation would have to take place at Paull in order for them to operate from there. Now flying from Kirmington and Paull, Humber Airways speciality was in offering short notice flights across the UK (mostly to London), Europe, Iceland, the Faroe Islands and Scandinavia; trawler companies sometimes used the service to fly their employees home or to other ports. Flights from the area were not a success though and Humber Airways ceased operations in January 1975. This failure for commercial flights didn't deter the Northern Pig Development Company from forming a new subsidiary called NPD Aviation in 1977. Using Piper Aztec five-seater planes they offered a charter service from Paull Airfield to businessmen, oilfield workers and fishermen. In the meantime the Hull Aero Club organized a whole range of public activities at the site, including air shows and one-off pleasure flights. On 4th May 1980 the Amy Johnson Air Pageant celebrated the 50th anniversary of Amy's flight to Australia and a crowd of over 4,000 spectators were entertained by 50 pilots in vintage airplanes. By early 1977 the airfield was occupying 152 acres of land at Oxgoddes and was given another five years of use although they still had to renew permission yearly from Holderness Borough Council.

The airfield became the home of the first production Beverley C.1 airplane (opposite), built by the Blackburn Aircraft Company at Brough, also the last Beverley to fly. Never used for "active" service by the RAF, it spent most of its working life at the Royal Aircraft Establishment at Farnborough, a training college for airmen before being moved to Paull for preservation. Having being bought by North Country Breweries Ltd., the plane was flown in to Paull Airfield on Saturday 30th of March 1974.[133] and the intention was that it would become the airfield's clubhouse. In September 1974 Holderness Borough Council granted temporary permission for this, renewed in 1977.

In 1981 the lease on Paull Airfield ran out and it was not renewed. The last plane to fly out of the airfield was a Cessna in early June; it had stayed on at the airfield to fulfill a pre-booked flight for Bransholme school children. NPD Aviation transferred its operation to Leeds Airport. The Beverley plane remained at the airfield for another two years until it was sold to a group of businessmen who wanted to scrap it. However, local entrepreneur Francis Daly intervened after much outcry about the plane's fate. He bought the plane then donated it to the Museum of Army Transport at Beverley (where it was opened to the public in 1987). When this closed it returned to Paull to be housed at Fort Paull Museum. The Hull Aero Club temporarily moved to Grindale, Bridlington, then to Brough in 1986 until finding a more permanent home in 1991 at Leven Airfield where the club still operates to this day.

References – Chapter 10

[130] *Hull Daily Mail*, 25th September 1959.

[131] *Hull Daily Mail*, 12th February 1960.

[132] *Hull and Yorkshire Times (City issue)*, 27th June 1969, p. 1.

[133] *Yorkshire Post*, 1st April 1974, and: Overton, Bill. *Blackburn Beverley*. Leicester, 1990, p. 145.

Chapter 11: Paull at the Start of the 21st Century

The 21st century sees many villages in decline, losing their employment, trades, shops, schools, church attendances and communities. Whilst the last shop in the village closed in the first decade of this century, Paull is far from declining. Thanks to refurbishments of the Royal Oak and the Humber Tavern the three historic public houses in the village are still thriving and finding new customers. Old trades are continuing too; a shipyard is still open and drawing crowds to see boats launched in to the Humber.

Hepworth's Shipyard with a boat almost complete.

Rusting hulks in the Humber off Paull belie the fact that shipbuilding still continues to this day.

Ship building.

View towards Hull. A docked North Sea Ferry can be seen in the background.

Paull's historic buildings are finding new uses to serve the community and draw people to them. With dwindling congregations, a decaying building needing a new roof and walls re-pointing the parishioners of Paull's 14th century church consulted the community about its future; the response was an overwhelming desire to save the church and several years of fundraising followed resulting in a match grant from English Heritage which has meant that the church has undergone significant refurbishment. It still holds services but also acts as a community centre for events and a café facility (open Saturday and Sunday afternoons in the summer) for visitors to the village.

The population of Paull remains healthy. Throughout the 20th century new housing continued to be built in the village with new streets bearing names connected to its history: Holme Close, Paghill Estate, Ferryman Park, Humber Villas. This continues today with the latest new housing completed in 2010 on the main street.

New housing.

Having been decommissioned in the 1950s Paull Point Battery has had several owners over the decades who have had varying ideas for its use including a holiday park and a theme park. However, in 2000 it opened as a military museum under the name of Fort Paull and it continues to attract visitors.

Entrance to Fort Paull Military Museum (formerly Paull Point Battery).

Operating the guns at Paull.

BIBLIOGRAPHY

General histories (including all subjects)

Bulmer, T., *History, Topography and Directory of East Yorkshire (with Hull)*, Ashton on Ribble, 1892.

Churchill, Winston S., *The Second World War, Volume I: The Gathering Storm*, London, 1948.

Clay, J.W., "Royalist Composition Papers II" in: *Yorkshire Archaeological Society Record Series*, vol. 18, 1895, pp. 139-140.

Department for Culture, Media and Sport, *Scheduled Entry for World War II Decoys for Hull Docks*, London, 2001.

Dobinson, Colin., *Fields of Deception: Britain's Bombing Decoys of World War II*, London, 2000.

Dorman, Jeffrey E., *Guardians of the Humber: a History of the Humber Defences 1856-1956*, Hull, 1990.

East Riding Registry of Deeds (held by East Riding Archives office, Beverley):

> High Paull House: HD 250 301, 4th August 1853; HD 252 302, 20th March 1854; ID 282 396, 13th March 1861; ID 60 74, 15th April 1864.

Hogg, Ian V., *Coast Defences of England and Wales 1856-1956*, Newton Abbot, 1974.

James Gairdner and R.H. Brodie, *Letters and Papers Foreign and Domestic Of the Reign of Henry VIII*, London, 1900.

Kent, G.H.R. "Paull", Allison, K.J. (ed.), *The Victoria History of the Counties of England: a History of the County of York, East Riding, vol. v, Holderness: Southern Part*, Oxford, 1984, pp. 11-127.

Major R. Saunders, *History of the 2nd East Riding of Yorkshire Royal Garrison Artillery (Volunteers) Hull*, Hull, 1907.

Miles, George T. and Richardson, William., *A History of Withernsea with Notices of Other Parishes in South Holderness in the East Riding of the County of York*, Hull, 1911.

Ministry of Information, *Roof Over Britain: the Official Story of Britain's Anti-Aircraft Defences 1939-1942*, London, 1943.

Nicholson, John., *Beacons of East Yorkshire,* Hull, 1887.

Norfolk, R.W.S. Militia, *Yeomanry and Volunteer Forces of the East Riding 1689-1908*, East Yorkshire Local History Society, 1965.

Poulson, George., *The History and Antiquities of the Seigniory of Holderness in the East Riding of the County of York*, Hull, 1841.

Sheahan, James Joseph., *History of the Town and Port of Kingston upon Hull,* 2nd ed., Hull, 1866.

White, Col. W. Lambert., *Records of the East Yorkshire Volunteer Force (1914-1919)*, Hull, 1920.

Willatt, William Henry., *This Incarnation: being Recollections of William Henry Willatt*, Malet Lambert Local History Originals, vol. 25, 1985.

Houses/Property/Architecture/Archaeology

Allison, K.J., *'Hull Gent Seeks Country Residence' 1750-1850*, East Yorkshire Local History Society, 1981.

Avery, Tracey., *Tattershall Castle*, National Trust, 1997.

East Riding Registry of Deeds (held by East Riding Archives office, Beverley):

> Boreas Hill: K 10 11; AB 268 470, 1st May 1760; AG 179 359, 31st May 1763; FN 243 242, 3rd July 1840; Vol. 47 319 296, 7th November 1891; vol.1094 12 12, 12th February 1958; vol. 1529 31 28, 2nd November 1967; vol. 1529 32 29, 2nd November 1967; vol. 1529 366 334, 17th November 1967.

High Paull House: HD 250 301, 4th August 1853; HD 252 302, 20th March 1854; ID 282 396, 13th March 1861; ID 60 74, 15th April 1864.

Paull Holme Tower: E 319 56, 4th January 1715; H 5 10, 5th April 1721; vol. 227 189 157, 11th January 1921; vol. 352 561 452, 31st August 1927.

Emery, Anthony., *Greater Medieval Houses of England and Wales 1300-1500, vol. I Northern England*, Cambridge University Press, 1996.

Hull Daily Mail, 21st August 1947.

Humber Archaeology, *Paull Holme Tower: an Archaeological and Architectural Survey*, Beverley, 1992.

Morris, Marc., *Castle: A History of the Buildings that Shaped Medieval Britain*, London, 2003.

Neave, David., and Waterson, Edward., *Lost Houses of East Yorkshire*, Georgian Society for East Yorkshire, 1988.

Pevsner, Nikolaus., and Neave, David., *The Buildings of England, Yorkshire: York and the East Riding*, 2nd ed., London, 1995.

Russell Studiocraft, *Preston Tower*.

Ryder, P.F., and Coleman, S., "Paull Holme Tower", *East Riding Archaeologoist*, Vol. 7, 1983, pp. 85-90.

Salter, Mike., *The Castles and Tower Houses of Northumberland*, Malvern, 1997.

Simpson, Douglas W., *The Building Accounts of Tattershall Castle 1434-1472*, Lincoln Record Society, Vol. 55, 1960.

Smith, Terence Paul., "Hussey Tower, Boston: A Late Medieval Tower-House of Brick", *Lincolnshire History and Archaeology*, Vol. 14, 1979, pp. 31-37.

Military/coastal defence

Clay, J.W., "Royalist Composition Papers II" in: *Yorkshire Archaeological Society Record Series*, vol. 18, 1895, pp. 139-140.

Norfolk, R.W.S. Militia, *Yeomanry and Volunteer Forces of the East Riding 1689-1908*, East Yorkshire Local History Society, 1965.

White, Col. W. Lambert., *Records of the East Yorkshire Volunteer Force (1914-1919)*, Hull, 1920.

Place names

Jensen, G.F., *Scandinavian Settlement Names in Yorkshire*, 1972.

Nicholson, John., *Place-Names of the East Riding of Yorkshire*, Hull, 1926.

Smith, A.H., *Place-Names of the East Riding of Yorkshire and York*.

Watts, Victor., *Cambridge Dictionary of English Place-Names*, Cambridge, 2004.

Religion

Neave, David and Susan., *East Riding Chapels and Meeting Houses*, East Yorkshire Local History Society, 1990.

Index

A

Airey, Wilfred	19
Airfield	67-69
Airplanes:	
-Auster	68
-Blackburn Beverley	69
-Cessna	69
-Condor	68
-Piper Aztec	69
-Rollason Condor	68
Albermarle, Stephen Earl of.	53
Anson Villas	26
Artillery	29-32
Aumale, Count of	60

B

Bannister:	
-Anthony	15, 18, 49
-Jane	49
Bastardy Orders	65
Battersby:	
-Anne	61
-Elizabeth	60
-George	60
-James David	60-62
-Maria	60
-Rachel Ann	61
Beacons	21
Benyngton, Richard	11
Bevrere, Drogo de	3
Blaydes:	
-Ann	48
-Benjamin	15, 48, 64
-Catherine	48
-C.B.	15
-Christopher	48
-Delia Maria	48
-Elizabeth	48
-Frances	48
-Harriet Elizabeth	48
-H.M.	15
-Hugh	15, 23, 48, 64
-Hugh Marvel	48
-James	48
-Kitty	48
Boreas Hill	17-19, 21, 32, 49

C

Brickyard	63
Bridlington Aero Club	68
Bristow Helicopters	68
Brodrick, Cuthbert	44
Brough	69
Buck, John	44
Bull Sands	32-33
Burghley, Lord	3
Burlison & Gryll	48
Campbell, James	38
Campling:	
-Ada	61
-Dorothy	61
Carvile:	
-Ann	48
-Francis	17, 49
-Henry	17, 42, 48
-Margaret	48
-Michael	49
-Susanna	49
Carvill	17, 49
Catholicism	53
Census:	
-1881	26
-Religious 1851	53-54
Charles, Ken	68
Clark, Margaret	60
Coastguard Station	40
Colquhoun, James Lieut.	49
Constable, William	15
Cordeaux, Rev. R.D.C.	42, 49
Cromwell, Lord Ralph	12
Curtis, Henry	39

D

Daly, Frances	69
Dawson, Rev. Joseph	44
Decoy Sites	34
Degaussing	33
Distillers Company Ltd.	67
Domesday Book	3, 14
Drummond, Archbishop	44

E

Earl, William	49
East Yorkshire Aero:	
-Company Ltd.	67
East Yorkshire Regiment	32
Ellerman Wilson Line	68
English Civil War	14, 42

F

Ferries	63
Fishing:	
-Boats	63
-Shrimp	63
Forster & Andrews	44, 48
Fort Paull Museum	74

G

Garnett, William	65
Glynne, Sir Stephen	42
Godwin Battery	32
Grimston, Dorothy	13

H

Haile Sands	32-33
Harrison:	
-James	44
-Roger	44
Hawker Siddely	69
Heathcote, Michael	67
Hedon Aerodrome	67
Hedon Haven	3
Hepworth's Shipyard	61, 71
Herring, Archbishop	43-44
Holderness Borough Council	69
Holme:	
-Alexander	13
-Betty	44
-Bryan, Colonel	14
-Charles Henry	14
-Christopher	13, 14
-Dinah	14
-Edward	4
-Henry	13, 14, 49, 53
-James Henry	14
-John	13, 14, 53
-Letitia	49
-Mary	53
-Penelope	49
-Robert	41, 53
-Stephen	14, 44
-Wilfrid	17
-William	53
High Paull	3, 23, 48
High Paull House	15-16, 18, 25, 26, 54
Holderness	3-4, 6, 11, 13
Hosdell:	
-J. Tuke	19
-R.J.	19
Howlett, John	67
Hull Aero Club	67-69
Hull Castle	21
Hull Corporation	67-68
Hull Docks	34
Hulme:	
-Dudley	64
-William	64
Humber Airways	68-69
Humber Anti-Aircraft Defences	33
Humber Conservancy Board	38, 40
Hussey Tower	11-13
Hutchinson, Thomas	14
Hutton Cranswick	67
Hutton, Dr. J.T.	44, 61

I

Iveson, Benjamin	14

J

Jenkins, Miss	49
Johnson:	
-Amy	69
-Herbert	14
Jones, Rev. J.S.	43, 47

K

Keyingham	44, 65

Kilnsea	32	Ombler:	
Kirby, Mary	65	-John	48
Kirmington	69	-Sarah	48
		Over Paull	3
		Oxgoddes	67-69

L

Lacy, "Ginger"	67		
Leven Airfield	69		
Liddle, William	65	Pagele	3-4
Lighthouses	36-40, 57	Paghel	3-4, 41
Lister, Anna	53	Paghill	4
Little Humber Farm	34, 67	Pagula	42, 53
Locke:		Parish Church:	41-53, 61, 73
-Barbara	47	-incumbents of	52
-Thomas	47	-interior of	46-51
Low Paull	3	-plan of church	45
		Patrington	66
		Paull Aerodrome	68

M

		Paull Church	13
		Paull Fleet	3
Marfleet	64	Paull Green	42
Martin, John	65	Paull Holme	3, 6-14, 41,
Marvel, Ann	48		49, 53
Medforth, Neville	67-69	Paull Holme Tower	6-14
Methodism:		Paull Point Battery	15, 20-34, 38,
-Hedon	55		43, 62, 63, 74
-North Cave	54	Paull Sand & Gravel Co.	14
-Primitive	53-55	Pease, Rev. George Clifford	43
-Wesleyan	53	Peck, M.C.	3
Moxon, George Dunhill	54	Pele Towers	6, 10-11
Museums:		Pier House	61
-Army Transport, Beverley	69	Poor Law Acts	65
-Battersby	60-62	Prickett:	
-Fort Paull	62, 69, 74	-George	18
Muster rolls	4	-Marmaduke	18
		Primitive Methodism	53-55
		Pryme, Peter de la	48

N

		Public Houses:	
		-Bunting, Montague	58
Napoleonic Wars	21-23, 63	-Crown	58, 65
Naylor, Gertrude	61	-Grapes	59
Newlands	67	-Haas, Mrs.	58
Newton Garth	3, 47	-Humber Tavern	23, 38, 57, 59,
Non-conformist chapels	53-55		65, 70
North Country Breweries	69	-Milsom, Elizabeth	57
North Killingholme	32	-Pickering, Mrs.	58
Northern Pig Development Company	69	-Royal Oak	57-58, 65, 70
		-Ship Inn	59
		-Stark, James	58

O

		-Watson, John	59

-Wright, Robert   57-59

Q

Quaker   44, 53
Queen Anne's Bounty   43

R

"Rabbit Nanny": see Jenkins, Miss
Race, Benjamin   55
RAF   68-69
Ridsdale, William   38
Robinson:
    -Dorothy   47
    -Leonard   47
Robson, Rev. William   43
Rochford Tower   12-13
Royal Aircraft Establishment:
    -Farnborough   69
Ryhill   65

S

Saint Andrew: see Parish Church
Saltend   64
Scott, Christopher   48
Seaplane Base   68
Ships:
    -Anson   63-64
    -Apollo   63
    -Proserpine   63
Simon, Frances   44
Skeffling   14
Smithson, Rev. John   42
Spurn Point/Spurn Head   22, 30, 32, 33
Stallingborough   23, 27, 32
Steemson, Thomas   63
Stephenson, Sarah   65
Stokesley, William   53
Storry & Jagger   39
Stovin:
    -Cornelius   18, 50
    -Frances Eth. Joanna   17, 49
    -James   17, 49
    -Margaret Susanna Maria   18, 49
    -Sarah-Anne   18, 49
    -Susanna   17-18, 49

-Susanna Maria   49
Submarine Mining   24-26
Sunk Island   32

T

Tattershall Castle   11-12
Thompson & Stather   39
Thorney Crofts   34
Thorngumbald   6, 17, 43, 65, 69
Thorngumbald Clough   38-40
Torre:
    -James   53
    -Manuscript   52-53
    -Nicholas   14
Trinity House   38, 57
Tudor:
    -Henry   13
    -Rose   13

U

Up Paull   3

W

War Department   15-16, 23, 26, 39
Wardale, John   68
Wastney, Elizabeth   13
Wesleyan   53
Willatt, William Henry   24-25, 29, 32
Winson, Thomas   40
Wood:
    -James   61
    -Richard   48
Workhouse   65-66
World War I   32
World War II   33-34, 67
Wray, James Lambert   48
Wrens   33
Wright, Horace Maylin Vipan   19
Wyton Bar   67

Z

Zeppelins   32